THE TEACHINGS OF THE MAGI

THE TEACHINGS OF
THE MAGI

A Compendium of Zoroastrian Beliefs

R. C. ZAEHNER

SHELDON PRESS
LONDON

First published in 1956 in Great Britain
by George Allen & Unwin Ltd

Published in 1975 by Sheldon Press
Marylebone Road
London NW1 4DU

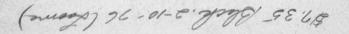

Printed offset in Great Britain by
The Camelot Press Ltd, Southampton

ISBN 0 85969 029 6 cased
ISBN 0 85969 041 5 paper

THE AUTHOR

R. C. Zaehner was born of Swiss parents who had emigrated to England and he was bilingual in French and English from early childhood. He remained an excellent linguist all his life. After school in Tonbridge, he went with a classical scholarship to Christ Church, Oxford, where he took a first in Oriental Studies. He lectured in Persian at Oxford University and served on the staff of the British Embassy in Iran for five years. He delivered the Jordan Lectures in London University in 1959 (later published as *Hindu and Muslim Mysticism*) and the Gifford Lectures at St Andrews in 1968–9. He was Spalding Professor of Eastern Religions and Ethics in the University of Oxford and a Fellow of All Souls College from 1952 until his death in 1974.

Cover illustration taken from a Sassanian carving on a rock panel at Persepolis showing Shapur being invested as King by Ohrmazd.

TO SIR MAURICE BOWRA

' . . . for an old friend is like old wine which becomes better and more fit for the consumption of princes the older it is' (p. 106)

CONTENTS

ACKNOWLEDGEMENTS

It is my pleasant duty to thank the Delegates of the Clarendon Press for permission to reprint extracts from my book, *Zurvan, A Zoroastrian Dilemma* in this work, and Mr. G. Morrison for assisting me in checking the translations from the Pahlavī.

All Souls College Oxford   R. C. ZAEHNER

INTRODUCTION

THE object of this little book is to present the general
reader with the main tenets of the Zoroastrian religion in
a short compass. By the 'main tenets' I understand the
teachings of the Zoroastrians on such fundamental subjects as the nature of God and the Devil, the genesis of
the universe, the reasons for its manifest imperfection,
man's situation in the universe, the purpose of religion
and the ethical system that follows on that purpose. This,
in turn, will lead us to consider their sacraments and
sacrifice, their beliefs concerning the fate of the soul at
death and their vision of the last things. By 'Zoroastrianism' I understand, arbitrarily, the dualist orthodoxy which seems to have been established under
Shāpūr II in the fourth century A.D. on which the surviving Pahlavī books are mainly based.

Thus the subject-matter of this book is the Zoroastrianism of the later Sassanian period as it has come
down to us in the so-called Pahlavī books. These books,
written in a language arbitrarily called Pahlavī, that is
Parthian, but which is in sober fact a dialect of Middle
Persian, were, in all cases in which a date is definitely
assignable, written after the Muhammadan conquest of
Persia in the middle of the seventh century. In matter,
however, they almost certainly go back to the reign of
Khusraw I (A.D. 531–578), and the orthodoxy re-
established during that reign in turn goes back to the
reign of Shāpūr II.

The Pahlavī books, on the whole present a consistent
corpus of religious doctrine. The qualification 'on the

whole' is, however, necessary. For though the fundamental dualist tenet that a good God could not be responsible for evil was never disputed, there did exist in Sassanian times a sect which sought to derive the two principles of good and evil themselves from a common non-moral and androgynous father who was Infinite Time. This heterodox sect is conventionally called 'Zervanite' because *Zurvān* is the Pahlavī name for the Genius of Time and because the Arabic heresiographers speak of the sect as the *Zurvāniyya*. Views emanating from this sect survive, often in a camouflaged form, in the Pahlavī books, but in the texts here selected for translation I have endeavoured to avoid those which show obvious traces of 'Zervanite' influence for the twin reasons that I have dealt with the doctrines of this interesting sect at some length elsewhere[1] and that, in this little work, I wish to present only the views of subsequent orthodoxy.

Zoroastrianism, as its name implies, is the religion founded by Zoroaster or Zarathushtra (to give him his proper name), the Prophet of ancient Iran. Around the figure of the Prophet, his date, and his place of origin furious controversy once raged and still simmers. This controversy is no concern of ours, since we are here concerned only with the fully developed orthodoxy of a much later time. Some account of the history of Zoroastrianism before the Sassanian period can, however, hardly be avoided. The following paragraphs, however, represent merely a theory, not a proven case; and the reader would do well to treat them with a decent circumspection.

The traditional date assigned to Zoroaster is 258 years 'before Alexander,' by which we may understand 'before

---

[1] Zaehner, *Zurvān, A Zoroastrian Dilemma*, Oxford, 1955 (ZZZ).

the death of Darius III in 330 B.C.'[1] This would give us the date of Zoroaster as 588 B.C. If we accept the tradition that by the date of Zoroaster is meant the year in which he converted King Vishtāspa at the age of 42, we can conclude that the Prophet was born in 630 B.C. The traditional date has, however, once again come under scholarly fire; and we must be content to say that we simply do not know when the Iranian prophet lived. However, we are not concerned here with the Prophet's date (since we are dealing with a far later form of his religion), but we are necessarily concerned with the surviving sacred books of the Zoroastrians known as the Avesta.

The surviving Avesta, which is only that fragment of the whole which is indispensable for the performance of the liturgy, falls into three distinct parts; and the disparity of these parts enables us to form some idea of the vicissitudes through which Zoroastrianism went before it became crystallized into a dogmatic religion during the reign of Shāpūr II. First we have the *Gāthās,* 'songs' or 'odes' which are generally and rightly ascribed to Zoroaster himself, secondly the *Yashts* or 'sacrificial hymns' addressed to various deities, and thirdly the *Vendidad* or *Vidēvdāt,* 'the law against the demons,' which is a treatise dealing mainly with ritual impurity and in which the dualism initiated by Zoroaster is carried to absurd lengths in the sphere of practical life.

The *Gāthās* give us the doctrines proclaimed by Zoroaster himself, but unfortunately linguistic science has only partially succeeded in eliciting the meaning from these obscure texts. The extent to which translators can differ is best illustrated by comparing the many translations of the *Gāthās* made by reputable

[1]See Henning, *Zoroaster,* p. 41.

scholars. The differences between them are startling. Yet despite the many obscurities of the *Gāthās* it is nevertheless true to say that the Pahlavī tradition, excerpts from which we offer in this book, is the natural continuation of the Gāthic doctrine: it is recognizably the re-affirmation of Zoroaster's own teaching as against the religion of the *Yashts* which represents a relapse into paganism.

In the *Yashts* we find a polytheism which is very similar to that of the great hymn-cycle of the earliest Indo-Aryans, the *Rig-Veda,*—a polytheism against which Zoroaster rebelled. Both in the *Yashts* and in the *Rig-Veda* we have a plurality of gods and demi-gods, and many of them have the same names. Thus in the *Rig-Veda* we meet with Mitra, Aryaman, Vāyu, Vāta, and Yama, and in the *Yashts* we have Mithra, Airyaman, Vayu, Vāta, and Yima. These gods and demi-gods succeeded in re-establishing themselves after the Zoroastrian reform, and in the *Yashts* they are very definitely 'high Gods,'—at least in the cases of Mithra and Vayu, —and not, as they subsequently became in the later Zoroastrian orthodoxy, what we would call 'angels.' Similarly we find entities which are important gods in the *Rig-Veda,* but which appear as demons in the Avesta : the principal among these are Indra, Śarva (Saurva), and Nāsatya (Nānghaithya). This was the direct result of the Zoroastrian reform, for all these gods are called *deva* in the *Veda,* and this name (*daēva*) they retain in the Avesta ; but in the mouth of Zoroaster and his successors this term means not 'god' but 'demon.'

Thus the Zoroastrian reform demonized that class of deity which was called *daēva* and eliminated the other class of deity called *ahura* by the Iranians and *asura* by the Indians with the single exception of Ahura Mazdāh (later called Ohrmazd) who was elevated to the status of the one true God from whom all other divinities proceeded. Over against this God stood Angra Mainyu (Ahriman), the Destructive Spirit; and life on earth is represented as a battle between Ahura Mazdāh and his attendant Powers on the one hand and Angra Mainyu and his demonic hordes on the other. For Zoroaster it was a very real battle since the worshippers of the *daēvas* were still the representatives of the traditional religion, and these he roundly identified with all that is evil. Among their practices seems to have been an animal sacrifice in which a bull was the victim; and this sacrifice Zoroaster vigorously attacks. In the *Yashts*, however, we again find repeated references to animal sacrifice on the grand scale. It is, then, clear that the state of religion existing in the *Yashts* represents a re-paganization of the Zoroastrian reform.

In the Pahlavī books, however, with which we are alone concerned in this volume, we find a return to the spirit of the *Gāthās*. The old Ahura Mazdāh, whose name has by now developed into Ohrmazd, is now the principle of good and Ahriman (Angra Mainyu) is the principle of evil. Neither the entities with which Zoroaster surrounded his supreme deity (the Amesha Spentas or 'Bounteous Immortals') nor the old gods later reintroduced into the system, are more than created spirits, subservient absolutely to the One Creator God. Similarly, in his own realm Ahriman is supreme and the other demons are his creations. Zoroaster's dualism has been systematized into a compact theology, and it is with this system that this little book is concerned. Apart from the Zervanite issue the only matter of controversy that still existed within the Zoroastrian 'Church' appears to have been that of animal sacrifice: this we shall have occasion to mention in our eighth chapter.

Thus it is the purpose of this book to present the

reader with an intelligible account of the main doctrines of the Zoroastrians; and in order that this may be done without bias I have selected a specific text or texts to form the kernel of each chapter. In this way it is hoped that the reader will be able to form a clear idea of the main Zoroastrian doctrines from their own words. In each case I have prefaced the text or texts with a short introduction in order to clarify or to emphasize particular points arising out of the texts themselves.

No translator with long experience of the maddening ambiguity of the Pahlavī script would claim finality for his translation. I have, however, confined myself to the easier texts; but when there is serious doubt as to the meaning I have added a note of interrogation (?). Where it has been necessary to emend I have shown my reading in a footnote without, however, giving the reasons which have led me to adopt a particular emendation. This may be vexatious to the scholar, but the nature of the series in which this book originally appeared precludes the introduction of elaborate philological footnotes.

CHAPTER I

A CATECHISM

As our first text we reproduce a short treatise entitled 'Selected Counsels of the Ancient Sages,' also known as 'The Book of Counsel of Zartusht.' Though the date is uncertain it seems likely that it was written after the fall of the Sassanian Empire, for the pessimistic utterances of §54 would seem to be a direct reflexion of the decline of the Zoroastrian 'Church,' that followed the terrible blow of the Muhammadan conquest.

The text sums up succinctly the whole of Zoroastrian doctrine : it is what every boy and girl of fifteen must know before he or she is invested with the sacred girdle, a ceremony which, coinciding with the age of puberty, may be compared with the Christian rite of Confirmation. It is, in fact, the Zoroastrian's catechism.

All religions necessarily start with man and his relationship to the world. So the first questions the catechumen asks are, 'Who am I? To whom do I belong? From whence have I come?' and 'Whither do I return?' The answers given in the rest of the text set out to situate man in his relationship to this world and the next, to God (Ohrmazd) and the Devil (Ahriman).

Man is, by origin, a spiritual being, and his soul, in the shape of what the Zoroastrians call his *Fravashi* or *Fravahr* pre-exists his body. Both body and soul, however, are creatures of Ohrmazd, and the soul is not eternally pre-existent as in many Eastern religions. Man, then, belongs to God and to God is his return.

Over against God stands the Devil, Ahriman. He, like God, is a pure spirit : he and Ohrmazd are eternal antagonists and sooner or later a struggle between them becomes inevitable. God (Ohrmazd) is all goodness and light, Ahriman all wickedness and death, darkness and deceit. We shall see later[1] how God is forced to create the universe as a weapon with which to defeat Ahriman. Creation is for him a necessity in his fight with the Fiend, and man is in the forefront of the fray,—not that he is driven to it by God, but because he freely accepts this role when it is offered to him.[2] On earth each individual is free to choose good or evil, and if he chooses evil, he is acting unnaturally because his 'father' is Ohrmazd[3] ; he is a son of God by nature being begotten of Ohrmazd and born of Spandarmat, the Earth.[4]

Thus for the Zoroastrians neither evil nor creation is a mystery. There is no problem of evil because it is a separate principle and substance standing over against the good God and threatening to destroy him.[5] There is, then, nothing mysterious about creation, for God needs Man's help in his battle with the 'Lie' as the principle of evil is frequently called in our texts. Being God's creation Man belongs to him, but God none-the-less depends on Man's help in order to defeat his eternal Adversary.

Evil is not by any means identified with matter as was the case with the Manichees. On the other hand, the material world is the handiwork of God, a weapon fashioned by the Deity with which to smite the Evil One. It is the trap God sets for the Devil,—a trap in which the latter is enmeshed and which so weakens him that in the end Ohrmazd is enabled to deal him the death-blow.

God is eternal, for 'Ohrmazd and the Space, Religion,

[1]Below, pp. 55ff.   [3]Below, p. 21, §2.   [5]Below, p. 36.
[2]Below, p. 41.   [4]*Ibid.*

18

and Time of Ohrmazd were and are and evermore shall be.'[1] Ahriman, on the other hand, has no beginning but has an end : 'he was and is, yet shall not be'[2] : 'he will be forever powerless and, as it were, slain, and henceforth neither the Destructive Spirit nor his creation will exist.'[3]

Both Ohrmazd and Ahriman are accompanied by subsidiary created spirits. Ohrmazd is helped by the six Amahraspands or Bounteous Immortals and by the *Yazatān* or gods, both of which roughly correspond to what we would call angels. Ahriman, on his side, is served by a host of demons, most of which are personified vices like concupiscence, anger, sloth, and heresy. The battlefield is this material universe created by Ohrmazd as a lure for Ahriman and in which Ahriman and his demons struggle for victory.

As this little text shows Man's role in this world is to co-operate with nature on the natural plane and to lead a virtuous life of 'good thoughts, good words, and good deeds' on the moral plane. Thus no religion has been as strongly opposed to all forms of asceticism and monasticism as was Zoroastrianism. It is man's bounden duty to take to himself a wife and to rear up for himself sons and daughters for the very simple reason that human life on earth is a sheer necessity if Ahriman is to be finally defeated. Similarly, no other religion makes a positive virtue of agriculture, making the earth fruitful, strong, and abundant in order to resist the onslaught of the Enemy who is the author of disease and death.

On the natural plane, then, virtue is synonymous with fruitfulness, vice with sterility : celibacy, therefore, is both unnatural and wicked. On the moral plane all the emphasis is on righteousness or truth,—for evil is personified as the 'Lie,'—and on the doing of good works in which Ohrmazd himself 'has his dwelling,'[4]—for, as

[1]Below, p. 35.   [2]*Ibid.*   [3]See ZZZ, p. 355.   [4]p. 24, §27.

the author of our little text sensibly remarks, deeds are the criterion by which alone a man can be judged.[1]

Such, then, is Man's place in the universal order and such are the duties he has to perform. Our text then goes on to summarize as briefly as possible the Zoroastrian doctrine of the future life. This is strikingly similar to Christian teaching, and it has been maintained, with some reason, that Christianity is here indebted to the 'Good Religion,' as the Zoroastrians habitually call their faith. At death the departed soul is judged by the gods: this is the 'three nights judgement' mentioned in §16. We shall have more to say about this in chapter IX.

At the end of Time men's bodies will be resurrected again and will participate in what is called the 'Final Body,' the restored macrocosmos from which all evil will have been expelled.[2] The transformation is brought about by the 'Sōshyans' or Saviour who appears at the end of time to initiate the reign of eternal beatitude after there has been a final purification of all souls, whether just or sinful, and when the denizens of Hell, having suffered the temporal punishment due to their sins, emerge again to partake in everlasting life and everlasting bliss.

With these few introductory remarks the text is best left to speak for itself.

SELECT COUNSELS OF THE ANCIENT SAGES
(*Pahlavi Texts*, pp. 41–50)

'(1) In conformity with the revelation of the Religion the ancient sages, in their primeval wisdom, have said that on reaching the age of fifteen every man and woman must know the answer to these questions: "Who am I?

[1] *Ibid.*, §24.   [2] Below, Chapter X.

To whom do I belong? From whence have I come? and whither do I return? From what stock and lineage am I? What is my function and duty on earth? and what is my reward in the world to come? Did I come forth from the unseen world? or was I (always) of this world? Do I belong to Ohrmazd or to Ahriman? Do I belong to the gods or to the demons? Do I belong to the good or to the wicked? Am I a man or a demon? How many paths are there (to salvation)? What is my religion? Where does my profit lie, and where my loss? Who is my friend, and who is my enemy? Is there one first principle or are there two? From whom is goodness, and from whom evil? From whom is light, and from whom darkness? From whom is fragrance, and from whom stench? From whom is order, and from whom disorder? From whom is mercy, and from whom pitilessness?"

(2) Now it is faith that searches out causes, palpable and as they are, and then, acting as mediator by means of reason (passes them on).[1]

So this must one know without venturing to doubt: "I have come from the unseen world, nor was I (always) of this world. I was created and have not (always) been. I belong to Ohrmazd, not to Ahriman. I belong to the gods, not to the demons, to the good, not to the wicked. I am a man, not a demon, a creature of Ohrmazd, not of Ahriman. My stock and lineage is from Gayōmart.[2] My mother is Spandarmat, (the Earth), and my father is Ohrmazd. My humanity is from Mahrē and Mahrānē[3] who were the first seed and offspring of Gayōmart. (3) To perform my function and to do my duty means that I should believe that Ohrmazd is, was, and evermore shall be, that his Kingdom is undying, and that he

[1] Translation uncertain.
[2] The Primal Man. See chapters II and III, below.
[3] The first human couple born of Gayōmart's seed from the Earth. See chapter V, below.

is infinite and pure; and that Ahriman is not, and is destructible; that I myself belong to Ohrmazd and his Bounteous Immortals, and that I have no connexion with Ahriman, the demons, and their associates.

(4) My first (duty) on earth is to confess the Religion, to practise it, and to take part in its worship and to be steadfast in it, to keep the Faith in the Good Religion of the worshippers of Ohrmazd ever in my mind, and to distinguish profit from loss, sin from good works, goodness from evil, light from darkness, and the worship of Ohrmazd from the worship of the demons. (5) My second (duty) is to take a wife and to procreate earthly offspring, and to be strenuous and steadfast in this. (6) My third (duty) is to cultivate and till the soil; (7) my fourth to treat all livestock justly; (8) my fifth to spend a third of my days and nights in attending the seminary and consulting the wisdom of holy men, to spend a third of my days and nights in tilling the soil and in making it fruitful, and to spend (the remaining) third of my days and nights in eating, rest, and enjoyment.

(9) I must have no doubt but that profit arises from good works, and loss from sin, that my friend is Ohrmazd and my enemy Ahriman, and that there is only one religious way. (10) (This) one way (is that) of good thoughts, good words, and good deeds, (the way of) Heaven, of light and of purity, of the Infinite Creator, Ohrmazd, who was always and will ever be. (11) (There is also) the other way of evil thoughts, evil words, and evil deeds, (the way of) darkness, and of the finiteness, utter misery, death, and wickedness which belong to the accursed Destructive Spirit (Ahriman) who once was not in this creation, and again will not be in the creation of Ohrmazd, and who in the end will be destroyed.

(12) I must have no doubt but that there are two first principles, one the Creator and the other the Destroyer.

(13) The Creator is Ohrmazd who is all goodness and all light : (14) and the Destroyer is the accursed Destructive Spirit who is all wickedness and full of death, a liar and a deceiver. (15) Equally I must have no doubt that all men are mortal except only Sōshyans[1] and the seven kings (who help him).

(16) I must have no doubt but that the soul (*jān*) will be severed (from the body) and that the body (itself) will be dissolved. (Nor may I doubt) the three nights judgement (of the soul at death), [the raising of the dead and the Final Body] the crossing of the Bridge of the Requiter, the coming of the Sōshyans, the raising of the dead and the Final Body. (17) I must (further) observe the law of chivalry (*ērīh*) and the Religion of the Ancients, and (I must) preserve my thoughts in righteousness, my tongue in truth, and my hands in doing what is good.

(18) With all good men I must observe the law of chivalry, (19) peace and concord in all good deeds I do. (20) In my dealing with the good (I must) always behave according to justice and the dictates of the Good Religion. (21) With whomsoever it may be, in past, present, and future time, I must act in a common virtue and in a common righteousness (*ham-dātastān*). (22) Good deeds performed for the sake of the Law are of a higher value than those performed for one's own sake, and by them is salvation most assured.

(23) I declare that I have received the Good Religion of the worshippers of Ohrmazd and have no doubts concerning it not for any bodily or spiritual comfort (that it may bring), not for a pleasant life or for a long life, nor yet because (I know that) my consciousness must needs part company with my body. I shall never apostatize from the Good Religion of the worshippers of Ohrmazd, and I have no doubts concerning it. I neither

[1] The Saviour who appears at the end of time. See below, pp. 142ff.

approve of nor respect other religions, nor do I lend them credence. (24) For it is plain that of thoughts, words, and deeds it is deeds (only) that are the criterion : (25) for the will is unstable, thought is impalpable, but deeds are palpable indeed, (26) and by the deeds that men do ⟨are they made known⟩.

In Man's body three roads have been laid out. (27) On these three roads three gods (*mēnōk*) have their dwelling, and three demons (*druj*) seek to waylay. In thought Vahuman, (the Good Mind), has his dwelling, and Wrath seeks to waylay ; in words Wisdom has its dwelling, and Heresy (*varan*) seeks to waylay ; but in deeds the Bounteous Spirit (Ohrmazd) has his dwelling, and the Destructive Spirit (Ahriman) seeks to waylay. (28) On these three roads Man must stand firm, nor may he give up his heavenly (*mēnōk*) reward for the sake of worldly goods, wealth, or earthly desire. (29) For the man who does ⟨not⟩ guard these three bastions within his body which I have mentioned,—his thoughts proceed from evil thought, his words from evil speech, and his deeds from evil deeds.

(30) Next must I be thankful; and by thankfulness (I mean gratitude) for that it is within my power that my soul (*ruvān*) may not go to Hell. (31) For when a man passes from the loins of his father into the womb of his mother, then does Astvihāt, ('the Dissolver of Bones' and demon of death), secretly (*mēnōkīhā*) cast a halter round his neck which for his whole life's span cannot be shaken off, not through the power of a good spirit and not through the power of an evil spirit; (32) but after he has passed away, that halter falls from off the neck of the man who is saved through the good deeds that he has done, but the man who is damned is dragged to Hell by that very halter."

(33) Whosoever is in the world must perform the office a certain number of times and must know what

sins (he is liable to commit) with hand or foot,—unless[1] he be deaf or dumb : in that case he cannot be accounted guilty. Should (a deaf or dumb man) perform (a religious office), then it should be the ērpatastān, and he should know the commentary on it.

(34) Fathers and mothers must teach their children this much concerning good works before they reach their fifteenth year. If they have taught them this much concerning good works, the parents may claim credit(?) for any good deed the child does; but if the child has not been (properly) instructed, then the parents are responsible for any sin it may commit on attaining majority.

(35) Be agreeable to good works and do not have any part in sin. Be grateful for good things, contented in adversity, long-suffering in affliction (astānak), zealous in the performance of your duty. (36) Repent of all your sins, and do not allow any sin that brings punishment with it to remain (unconfessed) for even a moment. (37) Overcome doubts (varan) and unrighteous desires with reason (khrat). (38) Overcome concupiscence (āz) with contentment, anger with serenity (srōsh), envy with benevolence (huchashmīh), want with vigilance, strife (anāshtīh) with peace, falsehood with truth.

(39) Know that Heaven is the best place, that the kingdom of the spirit (mēnōk) is the most pleasureable, that the mansions (dēh) of the sky are the most luminous, that Paradise (Garōdhmān) is a shining house, and the doing of good works brings great hope of the Final Body which does not pass away.

(40) So far as lies within your power, do not pay respect to evil men, for by commending what is wrong evil enters into your body and good is driven out. (41) Be diligent in the acquisition of learning (frahang), for learning is the seed of knowledge, and its fruit is wis-

[1]Reading 'bē 'kadh for 'bē 'kē.

dom, and wisdom rules both worlds. (42) Concerning this it has been said that learning is an adornment in prosperity, a protection in hard times, a ready helper in affliction (astānak), a *guide[1] in distress. (43) Do not make mock of anyone at all; for the man who mocks will himself be mocked, will lose his dignity (khwarr) and be execrated; and rarely indeed will he have a decent[2] or warlike son.

(44) Seek every day the company of good men to ask their advice, for he who makes a habit of seeking the company of good men, will be blessed with a greater share of virtue and holiness. (45) Go three times a day to the Fire Temple and do homage to the Fire; for he who makes a habit of going to the Fire Temple and of doing homage to the Fire, will be blessed with a greater share of both worldly wealth and of holiness. (46) Take great care never to vex your father and mother or your superior lest your body become ill-famed (thereby) and your soul see damnation.

(47) Know that of all the countless adversities that the accursed Destructive Spirit devised these three are the most grievous,—the obstruction of the sight of the eye, deafness of the ear, and thirdly the Lie of discord (anāshtīh). (48) For it is revealed that for this reason does the Sun issue his command to men on earth three times a day. (49) At dawn he says, "Ohrmazd ever bids you who are men to be diligent in the doing of good works so that I may bestow earthly life upon you." (50) At midday he says, "Be diligent in seeking out a wife, in the procreation of children, and in your other duties, for until the Final Body (comes to pass) the Destructive Spirit and his abortions will not be separated from this world." (51) At eventide he says, "Repent of the sins you have committed that I may have compassion on you."

[1]Reading pēshōpādh for pēshak.　　[2]Reading *shāyandak.

26

For it is revealed that just as the light of the Sun comes down to earth, so do his words come to earth.

(52) In this material world do not think, say, or do what is wrong (false) in thought, word, or deed. (53) Through the power of the gods, and by way of wisdom and by consultation with the Religion be vigilant and zealous (for good works), and consider that since the value of good works is so great and limitless, the Destructive Spirit strives his utmost to conceal (this truth) and to cause you misery, and Ohrmazd strives his utmost to reveal (the truth). Whosoever has knowledge of the Religion, let him be diligent in the doing of good works and be forever steadfast therein.

(54) At the end of this millennium when[1] the wickedness of the demons knows no limit and the Religion of Ohrmazd is much reduced and that of the unrighteous is predominant, when discussions concerning the Law and Religion between good and righteous men who know their duty have ceased, when the deeds of Ahriman and the demons are done openly,—and the sign of this will be that there will be a (general) retrogression when *creatures[2] will be destroyed, those who break contracts and who have taken the part of the demons and opposed the religion will go free, and when throughout the length and breadth of the lands which acknowledge the Law of Ohrmazd (all) good creatures will despair[3] on account of wicked tyrants (azhidahākān),—then every man must add to his (inner) peace through (the power of) Vahuman, (the Good Mind), consult with Wisdom through the Religion, search out the way of holiness by wisdom, rejoice his soul by means of generosity, show honour to rank by benevolence, seek a good name by manliness,

---

[1]Reading 'kadh dēv for 'kē dēn.
[2]Reading d⟨ā⟩mān for zamān against ZZZ, p. 236, n. 8.
[3]Reading ⟨an⟩ōmētīh.

collect friends by humility, make hope acceptable by long-suffering, store up (for himself) goodness by temperance (*khēm*), and prepare the way to bright heaven by righteousness; for there shall he enjoy the fruits of his good works.

(55) The body is mortal but the soul is immortal.[1] Do good works, for the soul is (real), not the body, the next world is (real), not this world. (56) Do not abandon the care of the soul and forget it for the body's sake. (57) Out of respect for persons (and out of forgetfulness) that all the goods of this world must perish, do not lust after anything that will bring punishment on your body and retribution on your soul. Desire rather those things whose fruit is an everlasting joy.

(58) Doing good is born of zeal, ⟨zeal⟩ of prayer(?),[2] prayer of desire, desire of intellect, intellect of knowledge of the other world; and knowledge (of the other world) is a weapon that was and is and (evermore) shall be. By it He is known Who creates all things anew, Who teaches (all) things, Who ordains all that should be done, Who wills the good (*sūt*) of all in this world and the next.'

[1] Reading *asachishn. [2] Reading *zhahishn*.

CHAPTER II

THE TWO PRIMEVAL SPIRITS
AND CREATION

THE story of the two primeval Spirits and the creation of the world is recounted in greatest detail in the first chapter of a ninth century book usually known as the *Bundahishn* or '(Book of) the primal Creation.' This survives in a longer and a shorter version. The text which we reproduce below follows the shorter version as far as §18 where it stops : from there on we follow the longer. It seemed better to confine ourselves in the main to the shorter version because it is straightforward and is the 'orthodox' account. Between §§15 and 16 the longer version, generally known as the *Greater Bundahishn,* interpolates a long passage which cannot be reconciled either with what goes before or with what follows. The confusion is appalling, and I have therefore refrained from reproducing it here. Interested readers will find a translation of this passage in my *Zurvān, A Zoroastrian Dilemma,* pp. 314–17. Even our present text is not wholly consistent as will shortly appear.

An apparent inconsistency appears right at the beginning. If Ahriman is an independent substance and co-eternal with Ohrmazd, it follows that Ohrmazd himself cannot be infinite since he is limited by his rival. This is clearly recognized in §4 where it is said that 'both Spirits in themselves are finite.' Yet in §1 it is stated that 'Ohrmazd and the Space, Religion, and Time of Ohrmazd were and are and evermore shall be.' The

29

contradiction, however, is perhaps only apparent, in that here Ohrmazd is identified only with infinite *Time,* not with *infinite* Space. In Time he is infinite, in Space, he is limited. Originally, then, he is eternal but not infinite,— unbounded by time, yet bounded by space which he must share with Ahriman and the Void which lies between the two kingdoms.

Ahriman, however, is bounded by both Space and Time. Spatially he is bounded on the upper side by the Void : temporarily 'he was and is, yet will not be.' Hence it was possible for the author of the text we reproduced in chapter I to say that 'Ahriman is not' (§3), for at the end of time he will be destroyed.[1] Ahriman is, then, spatially finite in that his domain extends to an unlimited extent in a downward direction but is bounded on the upper side by the Void ; and he is finite also in time since he and his kingdom will in the end be utterly destroyed. Ohrmazd is originally spatially finite, but ultimately infinite both in space and time, for with the destruction of Ahriman Ohrmazd is no longer spatially restricted : 'he knows the norm that exists between the two Spirits until the creation of Ohrmazd shall rule supreme at the Final Body for ever and ever ; that is the infinite.'

Thus in Zoroastrianism God is originally finite, limited as he is by the opposite principle Ahriman. So he would have remained for all eternity had not Ahriman been what he is, an Aggressor, and an ill-informed aggressor at that. The mere fact that Ahriman attacks makes it possible for God to become infinite, for this enables Ohrmazd to counter-attack in self-defence. It is the un-ordered attack of Ahriman that evokes the ordered defence of Ohrmazd, and it is the disorder in Ahriman himself that finally brings about his own overthrow. This story of the cosmic struggle results not only in the destruc-

[1] For what is meant by Ahriman's 'destruction' see pp. 143–4.

30

tion of Ahriman, but in the perfecting of an imperfect God : the good Spirit who was finite emerges as infinite. Ahriman, too, could have been immortal, had he so willed, but being the principle of death he could not will it so. Man, then, in fighting on the side of Ohrmazd, is fighting for his own immortality, his share in the Final Body which is the infinite.

So, in the beginning, the two antagonists are poised for battle, the one 'omniscient and good,' and the other the Aggressor 'whose will is to smite.' Ohrmazd foresees the attack and creates an 'ideal' or spiritual creation 'without thought, without movement, without touch' with which to defend himself, 'such creation as was needful for his instrument' (§5). One may well ask who or what this 'instrument' is. In fact it appears to be Vāy or the Void, for Vāy who appears both as a deity and as the Void is elsewhere described as 'the instrument he (Ohrmazd) needed for the deed.'[1] The Void, then, is enlisted by Ohrmazd in advance on his side. Creation and the Void are complementary, and once the battle begins, Vāy, the Void, is galvanized into life, it is the force which breaks down opposition, 'for he pursues the enemy from behind that he may smite the Aggressor and protect creation.'[2]

Meanwhile Ahriman is not idle. He has seen the light and would destroy it, so he sets about forging his own weapons in the shape of demons. Ohrmazd offers peace which is summarily rejected. As a compromise, then, the two Spirits agree to do battle for 9,000 years at the end of which, as Ohrmazd knows, Ahriman will be utterly destroyed.

So passed the first three thousand years of the great 'Cosmic Year' which lasts for 12,000 years. The battle proper begins with Ohrmazd chanting the *Ahunvar,* the key prayer of the Zoroastrians which corresponds, in the

[1]ZZZ, p. 316, §26.   [2]*Ibid.,* p. 333, §5.

importance they attach to it, to our own 'Our Father.' The mere recital of this prayer reveals to Ahriman that all is already over, and that his ultimate annihilation is certain. He swoons and falls back into the Darkness where he lies unconscious for three thousand years.

During Ahriman's indisposition Ohrmazd quietly proceeds to create the two worlds, the world of spirit and the world of matter. The two creations are complementary. On the spiritual side stand Ohrmazd and the six Amahraspands, the Bounteous Immortals, his arch-angels who are at the same time aspects of himself; on the other side stand Man and the six other material creations which are there to help him. Man himself is Ohrmazd's deputy on earth, for 'of material creatures he took to himself the Original Man.'[1] Each of the six Amahraspands also takes one of the material creations under his special patronage. The names of the Amahraspands are Vahuman (Good Mind), Artvahisht (the Best Righteousness or Truth), Shahrēvar (the Choice Kingdom), Spandarmat (Bounteous Right-Mindedness who is in fact identical with the earth), Hurdāt (Wholeness or Salvation), and Amurdāt (Immortality).

The six material creations are, in the order that they were created, the sky, water, the earth, plants, the Primal Bull, and Gayōmart, the Primal Man,[2]—and lastly fire which 'permeated all six elements.'[3] In the third chapter of the *Bundahishn* each of the Amahraspands adopts one material creation; Ohrmazd adopts Man, Vahuman cattle, Artvahisht fire, Spandarmat the Earth, Hurdāt water, and Amurdāt plants. Shahrēvar one would expect to adopt the sky, the only remaining member of the seven original creations. In fact he adopts metals which in our text are included in the creation of the earth. This discrepancy, however, disappears when we read that the

[1]ZZZ, p. 334, §11.   [2]*Ibid.*, p. 334, §8.   [3]*Ibid.*, p. 342, §25.

32

sky is made of 'shining metal that has the substance of steel.' Each material creation, then, stands under a tutelary deity. The two worlds are connected, and in close co-operation they both stand ready to face Ahriman again.

So far, then, there is no real inconsistency in this creation myth which is the orthodox Zoroastrian account. At this point, however, we meet with a distinct anomaly. We have seen that Ahriman was totally immobilized for three thousand years by the chanting of the *Ahunvar*. Yet in §16 we read: ' While Ahriman lay crushed Ohrmazd created his creation. First he fashioned forth Vahuman by whom movement was given to the creation of Ohrmazd. The Destructive Spirit first created the Lying Word and then Akōman (the Evil Mind).' How could Ahriman do this if he were unconscious?

I have suggested elsewhere[1] that during the first three thousand years of the Cosmic Year of 12,000 years Ahriman may have gained an initial victory,—at least in the unorthodox account of the so-called Zervanites who, as we have seen, differed from the orthodox in that they made Zurvān or Infinite Time the supreme principle and as such father of Ohrmazd and Ahriman. Now the discrepancy in our present passage seems to show that something has been altered in the original myth. Plainly Ahriman could not create the Lying Word, Akōman, the Evil Mind, and the other demons mentioned in §17 if he were totally unconscious as, according to our text, he was. The episode, then, must have been transferred from the first three millennia when Ohrmazd was content to create a wholly spiritual creation 'without thought, without movement, without touch' and thereby, one might have thought, singularly ill-adapted to resist any kind of attack whereas Ahriman fashioned some-

[1]*Ibid.,* pp. 99ff.

33

thing that seems far more effective,—'many demons, a creation destructive and meet for battle.' This demonic creation is surely the same as the demonic creation detailed later on. Moreover, the Lying Word is the exact opposite of the *Ahunvar,* the Word of Truth which Ohrmazd pronounces with such devastating effect.

Since, then, it would be impossible for Ahriman to pronounce the 'Lying Word' or to create his demonic creation while he was unconscious, we must conclude that this fearful falsehood was uttered and this unholy host devised at an earlier stage. But though there is evidence that in heretical Zoroastrianism this lie was as effective against Ohrmazd as the *Ahunvar* was later to be against Ahriman, given the text as we have it, we can only say that for the orthodox the lie in question must have been Ahriman's foolish boast in §9, 'I shall incline all thy creatures to hatred of thee and love of me.' In orthodox Zoroastrianism, then, Ahriman's first attack is the assault of falsehood, and it fails hopelessly because Ohrmazd knows it to be untrue and is therefore undismayed. He counter-attacks with the *Ahunvar,* True Speech, and thereby incapacitates Ahriman for a full three thousand years. During this period he fashions forth his own creation with which he will resist all further attacks. Ahriman's second attack will furnish us with the theme for our next chapter. For the present we will leave the *Bundahishn* to speak for itself.

BUNDAHISHN
chapter I (ed. Justi, pp. 1–3, Anklesaria, pp. 2–22)[1]

'(1) Thus is it revealed in the Good Religion. Ohrmazd was on high in omniscience and goodness : for infinite

[1]For an edition of this chapter, see ZZZ, pp. 276–321.

time he was ever in the light. The light is the space and place of Ohrmazd: some call it the Endless Light. Omniscience and goodness are the permanent disposition[1] of Ohrmazd: some call them "Religion." The interpretation of both is the same, namely the permanent disposition of Infinite Time, for Ohrmazd and the Space, Religion, and Time of Ohrmazd were and are and evermore shall be.

(2) Ahriman, slow in knowledge, whose will is to smite, was deep down in the darkness: ⟨he was⟩ and is, yet will not be. The will to smite is his permanent disposition, and darkness is his place: some call it the Endless Darkness.

(3) Between them was the Void: some call it Vāy in which the two Spirits mingle.

(4) Concerning the finite and infinite: the heights which are called the Endless Light (since they have no end) and the depths which are the Endless Darkness, these are infinite. On the border both are finite since between them is the Void, and there is no contact between the two. Again both Spirits in themselves are finite. Again concerning the omniscience of Ohrmazd— everything that is within the knowledge of Ohrmazd is finite; that is he knows the norm that exists between the two Spirits until the creation of Ohrmazd shall rule supreme at the Final Body for ever and ever; that is the infinite. At that time when the Final Body comes to pass, the creation of Ahriman will be destroyed: that again is the finite.

(5) Ohrmazd, in his omniscience, knew that the Destructive Spirit existed, that he would attack and, since his will is envy, would mingle with him; and from beginning to end (he knew) with what and how many instruments he would accomplish his purpose. In ideal

[1] Reading *khēmak* against ZZZ, pp. 286-7.

form he fashioned forth such creation as was needful for his instrument.[1] For three thousand years creation stayed in this ideal state, for it was without thought, without movement, without touch.

(6) The Destructive Spirit, ever slow to know, was unaware of the existence of Ohrmazd. Then he rose up from the depths and went to the border whence the lights are seen. When he saw the light of Ohrmazd intangible, he rushed forward. Because his will is to smite and his substance is envy, he made haste to destroy it. Seeing valour and supremacy superior to his own, he fled back to the darkness and fashioned many demons, a creation destructive and meet for battle. (7) When Ohrmazd beheld the creation of the Destructive Spirit, it seemed not good to him,—a frightful, putrid, bad, and evil creation: and he did not revere it. Then the Destructive Spirit beheld the creation of Ohrmazd and it seemed good to him,—a creation most profound, victorious, informed of all : and he revered the creation of Ohrmazd.

(8) Then Ohrmazd, knowing in what manner the end would be, offered peace to the Destructive Spirit, saying, "O Destructive Spirit, bring aid to my creation and give it praise that in reward therefor thou mayst be deathless and unageing, uncorrupting and undecaying. And the reason is this that if thou dost not provoke a battle, then shalt thou not thyself be powerless, and to both of us there shall be benefit abounding." (9) But the Destructive Spirit cried out, "I shall not go forth, nor shall I any more give aid to thy creation ; nor shall I give praise to thy creation nor shall I agree with thee in any good thing : but I shall destroy thee and thy creation for ever and ever ; yea, I shall incline all thy creatures to hatred

[1] This is presumably Vāy, the Void, which animates God's creation after it comes into existence.

36

of thee and love of me." And the interpretation thereof is this, that he thought Ohrmazd was helpless against him and that therefore did he offer peace. He did not accept but uttered threats. (10) And Ohrmazd said, "Thou canst not, O Destructive Spirit, accomplish all; for thou canst not destroy me, nor canst thou bring it about that my creation should not return to my possession."

(11) Then Ohrmazd, in his omniscience, knew that if he did not fix a time for battle against him, then Ahriman would do unto his creation even as he had threatened; and the struggle and the mixture would be everlasting; and Ahriman could settle in the mixed state of creation and take it to himself. . . . (12) And Ohrmazd said to the Destructive Spirit, "Fix a time so that by this pact we may extend the battle for nine thousand years." For he knew that by fixing a time in this wise the Destructive Spirit would be made powerless. Then the Destructive Spirit, not seeing the end, agreed to that treaty, just as two men who fight a duel fix a term (saying), "Let us on such a day do battle till night (falls)."

(13) This too did Ohrmazd know in his omniscience, that within these nine thousand years three thousand would pass entirely according to the will of Ohrmazd, three thousand years in mixture would pass according to the will of both Ohrmazd and Ahriman, and that in the last battle the Destructive Spirit would be made powerless and that he himself would save creation from aggression.

(14) Then Ohrmazd chanted the *Ahunvar,* that is he recited the twenty-one words of the *Yathā ahū vairyō* : and he showed to the Destructive Spirit his own final victory, the powerlessness of the Destructive Spirit, the destruction of the demons, the resurrection, the Final Body, and the freedom of creation from all aggression

for ever and ever. (15) When the Destructive Spirit beheld his own powerlessness and the destruction of the demons, he was laid low, swooned, and fell back into the darkness; even as it is said in the Religion, "When one third thereof is recited, the Destructive Spirit shudders for fear; when two thirds are recited, he falls on his knees; when the prayer is finished, he is powerless." Unable to do harm to the creatures of Ohrmazd, for three thousand years the Destructive Spirit lay crushed.

(16) While Ahriman lay crushed Ohrmazd created his creation. First he fashioned forth Vahuman (the Good Mind) by whom movement was given to the creation of Ohrmazd. The Destructive Spirit first created the Lying Word and then Akōman (the Evil Mind). Of material creatures Ohrmazd first fashioned the sky, and from the goodly movement of material light he fashioned forth Vahuman with whom the Good Religion of the Worshippers of Ohrmazd dwelt; that is to say that Vahuman knew what would befall creation even up to its rehabilitation. Then he fashioned Artvahisht, then Shahrēvar, then Spandarmat, then Hurdāt, and then Amurdāt.

(17) From the material darkness Ahriman fashioned forth Akōman and Indar, then Sāvul, then Nānghaith, then Tārich and Zērich.

(18) Of the material creation Ohrmazd ⟨fashioned forth⟩ first the sky, second water, third the earth, fourth plants, fifth cattle, and sixth Man.

(19) First he created the sky as a defence. Some call it "the first." Second he created water to smite down the Lie of thirst : third he created the all-solid earth : fourth he created plants to help the useful cattle : fifth cattle to help the Blessed Man : sixth he created the Blessed Man to smite the Destructive Spirit and his demons and to make them powerless. Then he created fire, a flame ; and

its brilliance derived from the Endless Light, a goodly form even as fire desires. Then he fashioned the wind in the form of a stripling, fifteen years of age, which fosters and keeps the water, the plants, and the cattle, the Blessed Man and all things that are.

(20) Now I shall describe their properties. First he created the sky, bright and manifest, its ends exceeding far apart, in the form of an egg, of shining metal that is the substance of steel, male. The top of it reached to the Endless Light; and all creation was created within the sky—like a castle or fortress in which every weapon that is needed for the battle is stored, or like a house in which all things remain. The vault of the sky's width is equal to its length, its length to its height, and its height to its depth: the proportions are the same and fit exceeding well(?). Like a husbandman the Spirit of the Sky is possessed of thought and speech and deeds, knows, produces much, discerns. (21) And it received durability as a bulwark against the Destructive Spirit that he might not be suffered to return (to whence he came). Like a valiant warrior who dons his armour that fearless he may return from battle, so is the Spirit of the Sky clad in the sky. And to help the sky (Ohrmazd) gave it joy, for he fashioned joy for its sake : for even now in the mixed state creation is in joy.

(22) Second from the substance of the sky he fashioned water, as much as when a man puts his hands on the ground and walks on his hands and feet, and the water rises to his belly and flows to that height. And as helpmates he gave it wind, rain, mist, storm, and snow.

(23) Third from water he created the earth, round, with far flung passage-ways, without hill or dale, its length equal to its breadth, and its breadth to its depth, poised in the middle of the sky : as it is said, "The first third of this earth he fashioned as hard as granite(?);

the second third of this earth he fashioned of sand-stone(?); the third third of this earth he fashioned as soft as clay." (24) And he created minerals within the earth, and mountains which afterwards sprang forth and grew out of the earth. And to aid the earth he gave it iron, copper, sulphur, and borax, and all the other hard substances of the earth except . . (?) . . , for that is of a different substance. And he made and fashioned the earth like a man when he tightly covers his body on all sides with all manner of raiment. Beneath this earth there is water everywhere.

(25) Fourth he created plants. First they grew in the middle of this earth to the height of a foot, without branches, bark, or thorn, moist and sweet: and every manner of plant life was in their seed. And to aid the plants he gave them water and fire; for the stem of every plant has a drop of water at its tip and fire for (the breadth of) four fingers before (the tip). By the power of these they grew.

(26) Fifth he fashioned the lone-created Bull in Erānvēzh in the middle of the earth, on the banks of the river Vēh Daitē, for that is the middle of the earth. He was white and shining like the Moon and his height was about three cubits. And to aid him he gave him water and plants, for in the mixed state he derives strength and growth from these.

(27) Sixth he fashioned Gayōmart (the Blessed Man), shining like the Sun, and his height was about four cubits and his breadth equal to his height, on the banks of the river Daitē, for that is the middle of the earth,—Gayō-mart on the left side, the Bull on the right side; and their distance one from the other and their distance from the water of the Daitē was as much as their height. They had eyes and ears, tongue and distinguishing mark. The distinguishing mark of Gayōmart is this, that men have

in this wise been born from his seed. (28) And to aid him he gave him sleep, the repose of the Creator; for Ohrmazd fashioned forth sleep in the form of a man, tall and bright, and fifteen years of age. He fashioned Gayōmart and the Bull from the earth. And from the light and freshness of the sky he fashioned forth the seed of men and bulls; for these two seeds have their origin in fire, not in water: and he put them in the bodies of Gayōmart and the Bull that from them there might be progeny abundant for men and cattle.'

With the completion of his spiritual and material creations Ohrmazd is ready for the coming struggle. At the same time, it appears, the souls or *Fravahrs* (*Fravashis*) of all men were created in the unseen world. Only if they would consent to descend to earth to carry on the struggle could Ohrmazd be assured of final victory. So Ohrmazd 'took counsel with the consciousness and Fravahr of men and infused omniscient wisdom into them, saying, "Which seemeth more profitable to you, whether that I should fashion you forth in material form and that you should strive incarnate with the Lie and destroy it, and that we should resurrect you at the end, whole and immortal, and recreate you in material form, and that you should eternally be immortal, unageing, and without enemies; or that you should eternally be preserved from the Aggressor?" And the Fravahrs of men saw by that omniscient wisdom that they would suffer evil from the Lie and Ahriman in the world, but because at the end (which is the Final Body), they would be resurrected free from the enmity of the Adversary, whole and immortal for ever and ever, they agreed to go into the material world.'[1]

[1]*Bundahishn,* Justi, p. 4; Anklesaria, pp. 38–9; ZZZ, p. 336.

CHAPTER III

THE DEVIL'S ONSLAUGHT

AHRIMAN's attack on the world of Spirit has failed, and
he has been thrown back into the darkness by the recita-
tion of the sacred formula. For three thousand years he
lies in a stupor, unable to move. The demons vainly seek
to revive him, 'but the accursed Destructive Spirit was
not comforted . . . for fear of the Blessed Man.' It is,
then, not only the magic power of the sacred formula
that keeps Ahriman at bay, but the First Man whom he
dare not attack, so holy is he. There now follows a very
strange episode which begins the text we reproduce in
this chapter and which is from the fourth chapter of the
Bundahishn.

Nothing the demons say or do can revive their stricken
captain until a character described as 'the Whore' makes
her appearance on the scene and boasts that she will
'take away the dignity of the Blessed Man.' At this Ahriman instantly revives, and the attack on the material
world begins. This, surprisingly enough, is the last we
hear of the 'demon Whore' whose intervention seems to
have been so very decisive. Another text, however, tells
us how she succeeded in corrupting the unfortunate
Gayōmart, the 'Blessed Man.' This text, from the *Selections of Zātspram,* tells us this:—

'When Ahriman rushed into creation, he had the
brood of the demon Whore of evil religion as his companion even as a man has a whore woman as his bed-
fellow; for verily the whore is a demon: and he

42

appointed the demon Whore queen of her brood, that is the chief of all the whore demons, the most grievous adversary of the Blessed Man. And ⟨the demon Whore⟩ of evil religion joined herself to ⟨the Blessed Man⟩; for the defilement of females she joined herself to him, that she might defile females; and the females, because they were defiled, might defile the males, and (the males) would turn aside from their proper work.'[1]

All this seems very un-Zoroastrian, for as we have seen in chapter I, the reproduction of the species is one of the first duties of man (p. 22). It is clear, however, from this and other passages that woman was held in slight esteem by the Zoroastrians, or at least by a sect of them,—for there are passages which exalt the virtues of the house-wife,—and that the reproduction of males, not of females, was the essential element in the defeat of the Evil One. Ohrmazd himself makes this quite clear in that he says:—

'I created thee whose adversary is the whore species, and thou wast created with a mouth close to thy buttocks, and coition seems to thee even as the taste of the sweetest food to the mouth; for thou art a helper to me, for from thee is man born, but thou dost grieve me who am Ohrmazd. But had I found another vessel from which to make man, never would I have created thee, whose adversary is the whore species. But I sought in the waters and in the earth, in plants and cattle, in the highest mountains and deep valleys, but I did not find a vessel from which blessed man might proceed except woman whose adversary is the whore.'[2]

It would seem clear, then, that the 'Whore' is the First Woman just as Gayōmart is the First Man. It seems that she was created by Ohrmazd and fled to Ahriman whose

[1] Zātspram, 34. 30–1 : ZZZ, pp. 350–1. See further *ibid.*, pp. 183–92.
[2] See ZZZ, p. 188.

consort she then became.[1] The Devil's kiss causes menstruation, a condition abhorred by the Zoroastrians as
being in the highest possible degree impure. Thus Man
is defiled by Woman and ever will be so till the final
Resurrection when both sexes are called to share in the
universal bliss. Through Woman who, though created by
Ohrmazd, chose to play the harlot with Ahriman, Man
and all his descendants are defiled. But Ahriman's victory
in this respect is only partial, for not only does the union
of man and woman make the reproduction of the race
of men possible, but woman remains forever subject to
man. As always the stratagems of Ahriman ultimately
turn to his own undoing.

Ahriman, then, revived by the demon Whore's
promise to destroy the dignity of the Blessed Man,
delivers his attack on the material creation of Ohrmazd.
He bursts through the periphery of the sky and rends it,
he defiles the waters and makes them brackish, he attacks
the earth by letting loose upon it all manner of filthy and
creeping things, he poisons the plants and brings disease
upon the 'lone-created Bull' so that he sickens and dies.
Next he attacks Gayōmart, the Blessed Man himself, with
the Demon of Death and 'a thousand death-dealing
demons' (§11), with 'concupiscence and want, with bane
and pain, with disease and lust and sloth.' Yet Gayōmart
is suffered by a decree of Time to live for thirty years
after the attack was launched. During these thirty years,
it must be assumed, his unholy union with the 'demon
Whore' was consummated.

Lastly Ahriman attacks the holy fire and befouls it
with smoke. At this point Ahriman achieves his highest
power. One thing, however, he had forgotten. Though
he had rent the sky and come upon the earth from its
lower side, the sky was able to close up the fissure and

[1]ZZZ, pp. 183ff.

44

Ahriman found himself entrapped in the material universe till the end of time. 'And the Spirit of the Sky said to the Destructive Spirit, "⟨Till⟩ the end of Time must I watch (over thee) so as not to suffer thee to escape" ' (5). Trapped then as he is in the snare of the sky, he is set upon by the powers of light until he and his demon host 'were routed and hurled into Hell' which is in the middle of the earth. Creation, however, has been definitively corrupted, and Ahriman remains within it to continue his abominable works until the Resurrection and the Final Body when all is made good 'and neither the Destructive Spirit nor his creation will exist.'[1]

BUNDAHISHN
chapter IV (Justi, pp. 5–6 : Anklesaria, pp. 39–46)

'(1) It is said in the Religion that when the Destructive Spirit saw that he himself and the demons were powerless on account of the Blessed Man, he was thrown into a stupor. For three thousand years he lay in a stupor. And when he was thus languishing, the demons with monstrous heads cried out one by one (saying), "Arise, O our father, for we would join battle in the material world that Ohrmazd and the Amahraspands may suffer straitness and misery thereby." One by one they minutely related their own evil deeds. But the accursed Destructive Spirit was not comforted, nor did he rise out of his stupor for fear of the Blessed Man, till the accursed Whore came after three thousand years had run their course, and she cried out (saying), "Arise, O our father, for in that battle I shall let loose so much affliction on the Blessed Man and the toiling Bull that, because of my deeds, they will not be fit to live. I shall take away their

[1]ZZZ, p. 355.

dignity (*khwarr*); I shall afflict the water, I shall afflict the earth, I shall afflict the fire, I shall afflict the plants, I shall afflict all the creation which Ohrmazd has created." And she related her evil deeds so minutely that the Destructive Spirit was comforted and, throwing aside his stupor, leapt forth and kissed the head of the Whore; and the pollution which is called menstruation appeared on the Whore. And the Destructive Spirit cried out to the demon Whore, "Whatsoever is thy desire, do thou ask, that I may give it thee."

(2) Then Ohrmazd in his omniscient wisdom knew that at that time the Destructive Spirit could give whatever the demon Whore asked and that there would be great profit to him thereby. The appearance of the body of the Destructive Spirit was in the form of a frog. And (Ohrmazd) showed one like unto a young man of fifteen years of age to the demon Whore; and the demon Whore fastened her thoughts on him. And the demon Whore cried out to the Destructive Spirit (saying), "Give me desire for man that I may seat him in the house as my lord." And the Destructive Spirit cried out unto her (saying), "I do not bid thee ask anything, for thou knowest (only) to ask for what is profitless and bad." But the time had passed when he was in a position not to give what she asked.

(3) Then the Destructive Spirit rose up together with his demons and his weapons to attack the lights. For he had seen the sky when it appeared to him in its ideal form before it was created in corporeal shape. In envious desire he rushed upon it,—and the sky was in the station of the stars,—and he dragged it down into the Void as I have (already) written above, for (the Void) lay between the first principles of Light and Darkness. One third of the sky was above the station of the stars on the inner side.

(4) (And Ahriman) leapt forth in the form of a serpent and trampled on as much of the sky as was beneath the earth and rended it. In the month of Fravartīn on the day of Ohrmazd at midday he made his attack. And the sky shrank from him in terror even as a ewe shrinks from a wolf.

(5) Then he came upon the waters which, as I have said, are established beneath the earth; and he bored a hole in the middle of the earth and entered in thereby. And he came upon the plants, and then upon the Bull and Gayōmart, and lastly he came upon the fire in the form of a fly. All creation did he assail. At midday he trampled upon all the world and made it as dark as the darkest night. He darkened the sky which is above and which is beneath the earth; and the Spirit of the Sky said to the Destructive Spirit, "⟨Till⟩ the end of time must I mount guard (over thee) so as not to suffer thee to escape."

(6) And upon the waters he brought brackishness (lit. "different taste"). And the Spirit of the Waters said " . . . (corrupt) . . . "

(7) And upon the earth he let loose reptiles in corporeal form,—and they mingled with each other,—reptiles, biting and poisonous,—the serpent-dragon, scorpion, venomous lizard, tortoise, and frog, so that not so much as a needle's point on (the whole) earth remained free from reptiles. And the Earth said, "May an avenger come upon these vengeful beings (in return) for this creation which they have created."

(8) And upon the plants he brought so much poison that in a moment they dried up. And the Spirit of the Plants said, "By the moisture[1] (that is his) Ohrmazd will cause the plants to grow."

(9) And upon the Bull and Gayōmart he brought

[1] Reading *tarrīh.

concupiscence and want, bane and pain, disease and lust (*varan*) and sloth. Before he assailed the Bull Ohrmazd gave him healing *mang* (Indian hemp) which some call *bang* to eat and rubbed it on his eyes, so that he might suffer less from the smiting and the wickedness and the torture. In a moment he weakened and sickened, but his pain was short-lived, for straightway he died. And the Bull said, "Let the actions and deeds (of men) consist in a perfect rulership over the animal creation."

(10) Before (Ahriman) came upon Gayōmart, Ohrmazd brought sleep upon him (lasting) as long as it takes to say a short prayer; for Ohrmazd created sleep in the form of a stripling of fifteen years of age, bright and tall. When Gayōmart awoke from that sleep, he saw the world was dark as night, and that on (the whole) earth there was not so much as a needle's point that remained free from the crawling of reptiles. The heavenly sphere began to revolve and the Sun and Moon to move, and the earth was all amazed(?) at the thundering of gigantic demons and their battle with the stars.

(11) Then the Destructive Spirit thought, "All the creatures of Ohrmazd have I made of no effect save (only) Gayōmart." And he let loose upon Gayōmart Astvihāt, (the Demon of Death,) and a thousand death-dealing demons, yet because of the decree of Time[1] they found no means of slaying him; for it is said that at the beginning of creation when Ahriman started to attack, Time extended Gayōmart's life and kingdom for thirty years, [he said] so that Gayōmart lived for thirty years after the assault was delivered. And Gayōmart said, "Now that the Aggressor has come, men will arise from my seed, and it is best for them to do good works."

(12) Then (Ahriman) came upon the fire and he mingled it with darkness and smoke; and the Seven

[1]Reading *zamān brīn*.

Planets together with many demons and henchmen mingled with the heavenly sphere to do battle with the constellations. All creation did he befoul even as if smoke were to rise from fire (burning) everywhere. And (these demons) corrupted the place of (the gods) on high and strove with them.

(13) For ninety days and nights did the spiritual gods do battle in the material world with the Destructive Spirit and the demons until they were routed and hurled into Hell. And the sky was made a fortress so that they could not mingle with it. Hell is in the middle of the earth at the point where the Destructive Spirit bored a hole in it and rushed in. So it is that in all the things of this world a dual operation can be seen, antagonism and strife, rising and sinking, and mixture everywhere.'

Ahriman has now succeeded in contaminating and defiling the whole of Ohrmazd's material creation. Though he himself has been cast into Hell, this is the hour of his greatest triumph. He is, however, reckoning without Ohrmazd's master-plan; for Ahriman, by breaking into the sky, has allowed himself to be caught in a trap from which he cannot escape; and the more he struggles, the more hopelessly enmeshed does he become. His predicament is described in the *Shikand Gumānī Vazār,* another of our Middle Persian books, where we find the Evil One compared to a noxious beast who unwittingly falls into a trap set for him by the wise gardener who is Ohrmazd.

SHIKAND GUMĀNĪ VAZĀR
chapter IV, §§63–80

'(63) (Ohrmazd) is like the owner of a garden or a wise gardener whose garden noxious and destructive beasts

49

and birds are intent on spoiling by doing harm to its
fruits and trees. (64) And the wise gardener, to save
himself trouble and to keep those noxious beasts out of
his garden, devises means whereby to capture them, (65)
like gins and snares and bird-traps, (66) so that when the
beast sees the trap and strives to escape from it, it is
ensnared inside it, not knowing (the nature of) the gin or
snare. (67–8) It is obvious that when the beast falls into
the snare, it is caught in it not because of the superiority
of the snare (itself) but because of (the superiority of) the
maker of the snare. (69) The man who is the owner of
the garden and maker of the snare knows in his wisdom
just how great the beast's strength is and for how long
(it can hold out). (70) The strength and power which the
beast has within its body is neutralized by its own
struggles and is expended in the proportion that it has
enough power to trample on the snare and to rend the
gin and to strive to destroy it. (71) Since its strength is
insufficient, its power to resist diminishes and it is put out
of action. Then the wise gardener, putting his plan into
effect and knowing (the needs of) his own produce,
drives the beast out of the snare; and the beast's substance remains but its faculties are put out of action.
(72) And the gardener returns his snare and gin un-
damaged to his store-house where he will refit it.

(73) So the Creator Ohrmazd, the Saviour of his
creatures and Ordainer of creation, the (God) who puts
the Principle of Evil out of action is like ⟨a gardener⟩
who protects his garden from what is harmful to it. (74)
And that noxious beast which ruins the garden is the
accursed Ahriman who disrupts and assails creation.
(75) The goodly snare is the sky in which the good creations are (like) guests, (76) and in which the Destructive
Spirit and his abortions are entrapped. (77) And the gin
and trap which prevents the noxious beast from achiev-

ing its desire (78) is the time set for the battle with Ahriman and his powers and weapons (known as) Time of the long Dominion, (79) which, by struggling with the beast in the gin and snare, destroys its power. (80) Only the Creator of creation (himself) can bring about again the salvation of his ⟨creatures⟩ from eternal adversity and can reconstitute its goodly progress, just as the wise owner of the garden (reconstitutes) his gin and snare.'

THE NECESSITY OF DUALISM

AHRIMAN'S shortlived triumph after his assault on Ohrmazd's material creation, the first stage in the cosmic battle between the two primeval Spirits, is now over: and this would seem a good moment to pause for a while to consider the philosophical basis on which Zoroastrian dualism rests.

The principal philosophical Zoroastrian text that has survived is the *Dēnkart,* a sizeable corpus of theological, mythological, and exegetic material dating from the ninth century A.D. The text of this work, however, is so difficult and corrupt that it would serve no useful purpose to reproduce any large portion of it in a work that is primarily intended for a non-specialist public. We will, then, again turn to the *Shikand Gumānī Vazār* the text of which is in a far better state of preservation and which presents the arguments in favour of a dualist solution to the cosmic riddle both clearly and well.

The author, Mardān-Farrukh by name, who lived well after the Muhammadan conquest at a time when to be a Zoroastrian involved political disabilities, was a Zoroastrian not so much because this was the religion of his Iranian forbears, as because he was convinced that it was the true religion. In the tenth chapter of the *Shikand*[1] he says: 'Now, as I have said above, I have always been earnestly anxious to know God and have been curious in searching out his religion and his will.

[1] §§43–60.

In this spirit of enquiry I have travelled to foreign countries and (even) to India and have frequented many sects : for I did not choose my religion simply because I inherited it, but I wanted (only that religion) which was mostly firmly based on reason and evidence and which was most acceptable (on these grounds). So I frequented many different sects until, by the grace of God and the power and glory and strength of the Good Religion, I escaped from the abyss of darkness and of doubts that were with difficulty dispelled. By the force of this religious knowledge . . . I was saved from much doubt and from the sophistries, deceptions, and evils of the sects, and particularly from that greatest and most monstrous of deceivers, the worst of false teachers, the "intellectually intoxicated"[1] Mānī.'

Mardān-Farrukh, then, was a Zoroastrian by conviction, and he was confirmed in this religion because it seemed to him to offer the only reasonable explanation for those perennial religious enigmas, creation and the undoubted existence of evil. From the seventh to the tenth chapters of his *Shikand* he marshals his arguments in favour of a dualist solution.

It is no accident that he singles out the religion of Mānī for his especial condemnation though, at first sight, this may seem strange. For Manichaeanism is as uncompromisingly dualistic as is Zoroastrianism,—but with what a difference ! Manichaeanism equates evil with matter, good with spirit, and is therefore particularly suitable as a doctrinal basis for every form of asceticism and many forms of mysticism. It profoundly affected Islamic mysticism, and through St. Augustine has left traces in Christianity itself. Its basic doctrine that this world was constructed from the substance of Satan was

[1] Reading *raimast* in accordance with the Manichaean texts for *rat-mastarag*.

profoundly abhorrent to the Zoroastrians whose attitude to the things of this world was essentially what William James called 'healthy-minded.' Zoroastrianism and Manichaeanism, as religious types, stand at opposite poles: they are both, in their own way, extremes. Zoroastrianism sees the whole physical creation as in itself good; what corruption there is was subsequently introduced by Ahriman, as we have seen. The world of spirit is the exemplar of this world but not essentially different from it; and the future life is a *natural* paradise in which there is neither death nor old age nor disease nor any of the things that make life on earth difficult and tedious. These evils are finally destroyed in the last days when Ahriman is either annihilated or totally incapacitated. For the Zoroastrian the body has its own essential dignity, inferior, it is true, to that of the soul, but dignity none the less. The Manichaean view that the body is composed of the substance of evil, that it is a prison and a carcase, is, to the Zoroastrian, unnatural, perverted, and blasphemous. Thus because the Zoroastrian sees man not as an immortal soul imprisoned in a mortal and diabolical body but as a harmonious whole the unity of which is temporarily disrupted by death, but fully restored and glorified at the final Resurrection, he is bitterly averse to any form of asceticism and has, as a matter of historical fact, never developed any form of mysticism. For him there is no dualism of matter and spirit; there is only a dualism of good and evil which is quite another matter. His hatred of the Manichee is instinctive and profound and, given the dogmas of each, absolutely reasonable.

His opposition to Islam and Christianity is on quite other grounds: they are not reasonable. For not only is he thoroughly at home in this world, he also dislikes mysteries and mystification. Further it is no accident that he himself calls his religion 'the Good Religion,' for there is one dogma on which he firmly takes his stand,—God is good. According to the Zoroastrian the Moslem God is not good, neither does he pretend to be, while the Christian God advertises Himself as Good, and plainly is not. Once you admit the reality of evil, then God is responsible for it unless Evil is an eternal principle co-existent with God and irreconcileably opposed to Him. Evil is not a privation as the Christians would have it, but a substance, and it does not need, therefore, to be explained away. It is not the world, nor even of the world, as the Manichaeans hold; it is rather a pure spirit, the negation of life, and naked aggression; it is wrong-mindedness, stupidity, blind self-assertiveness, error. There is no unity in the Cosmos as it is, nor is there unity in eternity. How could there be? since evil is a fact, not a problem. The Zoroastrians claim to face the fact rationally, and it is because they have consistently done so that they have not survived as a world religion, for 'religions are based on certain fundamental assumptions which, of their nature, do not admit of logical proof,'[1] and one of these is the unity of the creative principle. This Zoroastrianism flatly denies.

If, then, one accepts a fundamental duality in Being itself, the classic problems of religion disappear. Evil exists from all eternity : it is aggressive by nature and the good principle who is omniscient must, therefore, defend himself against it. There is no mystery about creation either.

'David said, "O king, since thou hadst no need of us,
Say, then, what wisdom was there in creating the two worlds?"
God said to him, "O temporal man, I was a hidden treasure;

[1] Zaehner, *Foolishness to the Greeks*, p. 10.

I sought that that treasure of loving-kindness and bounty should be revealed".[1]

So said the Moslem mystic, Jalāl-al-Dīn Rūmī. Pure verbiage to the Zoroastrian. God needs his creation as much as creation needs God, for his creation is his defence against Ahriman. Monotheism cannot 'explain' creation. There is no straight answer to the enigma of why a perfect and self-sufficing Being should create an imperfect world in which his creatures, as often as not, suffer torment. On the other hand 'creation' can be 'explained' as a hard necessity if God has to protect himself against a pitiless enemy who is co-existent with himself. God did not, according to the Zoroastrians, bungle his creation, nor does he 'repent' of it as Yahweh habitually does: he devised it as a trap in which to ensnare his enemy and as a machine in which the latter would be finally destroyed. He foresaw that Ahriman would temporarily corrupt his whole creation, including Man, his masterpiece; and foreseeing this and because he is good he did not send Man into the front line without first obtaining his consent. Man is the instrument of his victory and through Man's co-operation with God the Adversary is finally and utterly overthrown. Man suffers at the hands of Ahriman but at least he has the comfort of knowing that he is not being tormented by an all-powerful Being who is his own creator. The Zoroastrian does not know the predicament of Job.

God is good: that is the first Zoroastrian dogma, and to this Mardān-Farrukh returns again and again. In the chapter a translation of which follows, he develops three main lines of thought. First the existence of good and evil is empirically verifiable and this dichotomy is traceable to first causes. Secondly since God is by definition a rational (and omniscient) being his creation must have a

[1] R. A. Nicholson, *Divān i Shams i Tabrīz*, p. 15.

rational motive. Thirdly, if it is admitted that God is good, then it necessarily follows that evil cannot proceed from Him, however indirectly.

Good and evil, he argues, are contrary realities just as much as are darkness and light, fragrance and stench, sickness and health, and so on. They are differing and antagonistic *substances,* not merely different in the function they have to perform as, for example, are the opposites of male and female. This is shown by the fact that they cannot co-exist and are mutually destructive. Mardān-Farrukh then goes on to argue that since good and evil are demonstrable facts in the material world and since the latter derives from a spiritual or unseen prototype, it follows that there is a dichotomy in that world too,—a dichotomy that leads inevitably to two first causes which are mutually antagonistic and irreconcileable.

Now, granted that there are two independent principles one of which is by nature aggressive and the other of which is by nature pacific and wise, it follows that the wise principle will do everything in its power to ward off the attack which cannot fail to materialize. God, moreover, is wholly good, and it is therefore impossible that any goodness can be added to him : he is not capable of improvement or increase. He is, moreover, also a rational Being, and the actions of rational beings are motivated either by a desire to obtain a good which is not yet theirs, or to repel a hurt. The universe is a fact, and according to Zoroastrian dogma it is not eternal but has an origin, and it is God who has originated it, not Ahriman. Therefore, since God is a rational Being, it follows that it can only have been created in order to repel the injury that God might himself suffer from Ahriman's malice. Thus creation is God's plan for bringing evil to nought, and with the destruction of the evil principle God can become 'all in all,' which he never was before. For, according to the Zoroastrians, God, though perfectly good, is not infinite, for he is limited by the contrary principle. The good, though not susceptible of any addition, could nevertheless be harmed and therefore diminished by the onslaught of evil. So God exteriorizes the spiritual and material worlds from himself, ensnares Ahriman in this 'exteriorization' which is his creation and destroys him in it. Ahriman, when the battle is over, is not destroyed as a substance,—for a substance is by definition indestructible,—but he is, to use the Pahlavī word *a-kār-ēnīt*, he is 'put out of action' or 'deprived of actuality' : he is relegated to an eternal potency which can never be actualized again, or in more everyday language for people unfamiliar with the Aristotelian jargon, 'they drag Ahriman outside the sky and cut off his head.'[1] Only so does Ohrmazd himself achieve wholeness and infinity, 'for so long as evil is not annihilated, he whose will is good has not perfectly fulfilled what he wills' (§56).

Mardān-Farrukh's last argument used to demonstrate that God cannot, however indirectly, originate evil, is that a perfect being cannot originate what is imperfect. The imperfection that undoubtedly exists in creation must then be due to an agency other than God, and that is Ahriman. Were God capable of producing anything imperfect, it would imply imperfection in himself, and he should not therefore 'be worshipped as God or as perfectly good' : in fact by ceasing to be perfectly good he ceases to be God.

This, then, is the case for Zoroastrian dualism. Its great merit is that it absolves God from any breath of evil and explains how it could be that creation was actually necessary. It stands wholly opposed to Islam

[1] ZZZ, p. 183, n. 2.

which was to supersede it and there could not really be any *modus vivendi* between the two, since Zoroastrianism stands squarely on the goodness of God and cares not at all for his unity whereas Islam asserts above all things the absolute unity and unicity of God, his absolute transcendance and total incomprehensibility; and since the Moslem God is as capable of leading astray as he is of guidance, it is no accident that among his ninety-nine names that of 'good' is absent. The Zoroastrian God is reasonable as well as good; there is nothing 'numinous' about him. Ohrmazd and Allah are not compatible, and inevitably the good God of reason was forcibly ejected by the *mysterium tremendum* imported by the Semites.

SHIKAND GUMĀNĪ VAZĀR
chapter VIII

'(1) Another proof that a contrary principle exists is (2) that good and evil are observable in the world, (3) and more particularly in so far as both good ⟨and bad⟩ conduct are defineable as such, (4) as are darkness and light, (5) right knowledge and wrong knowledge, (6) fragrance and stench, (7) life and death, (8) sickness and health, (9) justice and injustice, (10) slavery and freedom, (11) and all the other contrary activities which indisputably exist and are visible in every country and land at all times; (12) for no country or land exists, has existed, or ever will exist (13) in which the name of good and evil and what that name signifies has not existed or does not exist. (14) Nor can any time or place be mentioned in which good and evil change their nature essentially.

(15) There are also other contraries whose antagonism is not ⟨one of essence but⟩ one of function, species, or

59

nature. (16) Such is the mutual antagonism of things of like nature as (for example) male and female, (17) (the different) scents, tastes and colours; the Sun, Moon, and stars whose dissimilarity is not one of substance but one of function, nature, and constitution, each being adapted to its own particular work. (18) But the dissimilarity of good and evil, light and darkness, and other contrary substances is not one of function but one of substance. (19) This can be seen from the fact that their natures cannot combine and are mutually destructive. (20) For where there is good, there cannot possibly be evil. (21) Where light is admitted, darkness is driven away. (22) Similarly with other contraries, the fact that they cannot combine and are mutually destructive is caused by their dissimilarity in substance. (23) This substantial dissimilarity and mutual destructiveness is observable in phenomena in the material world.

(24) The material world is the effect of the spiritual, and the spiritual is its cause, (25) for the effect is understood through the cause. (26) That the former gives testimony of the latter is obvious to any expert in these matters. (27) That the material is an effect and the spiritual the cause can be proved by the fact that (28) every visible and tangible thing emerges from an unmanifest to a manifest state. This is perfectly clear. (29) Thus man and all other visible and tangible creatures are known to proceed from the spiritual world which is invisible and intangible. (30) So too the mass, shape, length, and breadth (of a man) are those of his parent. (31) The body of man and of other creatures is the manifestation which derives from the unmanifest and invisible thing which is in the seed of their fathers, (32) and the seed itself which was in the fathers' loins becomes manifest, visible, and tangible. (33) So we must know with a necessary knowledge that this visible and tangible

material world was created from an invisible and intangible spiritual world and had its origin there. (34) Similarly there can be no doubt that the visible and tangible (material world) indicates the existence of an invisible and intangible world which is spiritual.

(35) Since we have seen that in the material world contrary substances exist and that they are sometimes mutually co-operative and sometimes mutually destructive, so (must it also be) in the spiritual world (36) which is the cause of the material, (37) and material things are its effects. That this is so is not open to doubt (38) and follows from the very nature of contrary substances. (39–40) I have shown above that the reason and occasion for the wise activity of the Creator which is exemplified in the creative act is the existence of an Adversary. (41) For it is a known fact that activity proceeds from an agent in two ways; it is either voluntary or natural. (42) The voluntary is of three kinds. (43) Two kinds are attributable to knowing and wise (agents), (44) (that is) either actions aimed at appropriating what is advantageous and good (45) or (actions) aimed at repelling and warding off what is disadvantageous and harmful and (which comes) from an external source. (46) One kind is attributable to agents of perverted intellect who are without (real) knowledge. (47) Such actions are haphazard and irrational. (48) Actions proceeding from knowing and wise persons cannot be irrational or unmotivated.

(49) Since the wise, omniscient, and omnipotent Creator is self-sufficing, his perfection consists in his having no need for any advantage or increase which he might desire from outside. (50) So we must conclude that the reason and the occasion for his actions must all be of one kind, (51) (namely) to repel and ward off whatever damage might accrue to him from an external

adversary who could harm him; and this is the whole reason and occasion for the act of creation.

(52) This too (must be considered): the wise Creator desires (only) what is good; (53) his will is wholly good, (54) and his creative activity is in accordance with his will, (55) and the will of a wise One who wills only what is good can only achieve its full fruition by destroying and annihilating evil; (56) for so long as evil is not annihilated, he whose will is good has not perfectly fulfilled what he wills.

(57) Now the goodness of the wise Creator can be inferred from the act of creation and from the fact that he cherishes and protects (his creatures), that he ordains and teaches a way and method by which evil can be repelled and sin averted, (58–60) and that he repels and wards off the Adversary who attacks the body; (it can be inferred too) from the organs and faculties of the body (afflicted as they are) by pain and sickness (which come to them) from outside and (which also are) inside[1] the body. All animals and plants are sustained and brought to fruition and made to increase by the sustaining and nutritive power called in Religion the *Fravahr* which co-operates with nature (61) and by the four assimilative (?) faculties, the attractive, retentive, digestive, and excretory. (62) Through the Creator's great wisdom these faculties co-operate harmoniously in repelling all manner of pain and sickness (brought on) by the Adversary who strikes at random and whose will is evil. (63) There are other faculties too which co-operate. (From all this) it can be concluded that the Creator wills (only) what is good.

(64) It is suffering and death that destroy the body, not the Creator whose will is good and who preserves and maintains the body. (65) This is clearly so because a wise

[1]Reading *nihąn* for *vahąn*.

Creator does not regret or repent of what he has done, (66) nor does he destroy his creatures or make them of no effect, (67) for he is wise and omniscient. (68) It is only possible to attribute regret and repentance for what one has done to one whose knowledge is defective, whose reason is imperfect, and who is ignorant of the final outcome, (69) for knowing and wise persons do not commit actions without cause or occasion. (70) Similarly the actions of ignorant men of perverted intelligence who are ignorant of the final outcome will be haphazard, without cause or occasion.

(71) But the wise (Creator) will dispose wisely and act in accordance with discrimination in warding off from his creatures (the Adversary) whose actions are haphazard and who does not know the final outcome. (72) He, the (demon) whose actions are haphazard, is walled up and circumscribed within a trap[1] and a snare; (73) for it is plain that a moving and living substance cannot be warded off or destroyed[2] in an infinite void, nor is there any security against his harmfulness (74) unless he is circumscribed, uprooted,[3] and made captive. (75) When he is circumscribed and made captive, he is susceptible to suffering and heavy chastisement. (76) But until he is completely conscious of his suffering and fully aware that his actions are based on a wrong knowledge, he continues to have utterly false views of what has befallen him. (77) His experience of suffering (is due to) the complete power of the omnipotent Creator.

(78) When once he has reached full realization of what he suffers at the hands of omnipotence, the wise Creator puts him out of action and hurls him into the infinite Void. (79) Then the good creation will have no fear of

[1]Reading *nivandak* (ZZZ, p. 218) for *niwə̄*.
[2]Reading *abhsihēnītan* for *awə̄fsūidan*.
[3]*Farahīdaa* = New Persian *parkhīda*.

him; it will be immortal and free from adversity. (80) Perfect is the wisdom and discrimination of the omniscient Creator of the good and (perfect is) his foreknowledge of what needs to be done.

(81) The dissimilarity of things is proved by looking at them. (82) Dissimilarity is of two kinds as has been stated above; (83) one is dissimilarity in function, the other dissimilarity in substance. (84) Dissimilarity of function involves co-operation and likeness of faculties, (85) but dissimilarity of substance involves incompatibility and opposition. (86) It is obvious that ⟨substantially dissimilar⟩ things cannot co-exist in one place. (87) If (all) things were one, this One would be nameless, (88) for it is only through the possession of a name that one thing can be distinguished from another. (89) That evil is principially distinct from good can be inferred from the fact that neither is the cause of the other. (90) That each exists in and by its own essence (91) is proved by the eternal antagonism and opposition between the two.

(92) If it should be objected that since there is a multiplicity of contraries (93) e.g. good and evil, darkness and light, fragrance and stench, life and death, sickness and health, pleasure and pain (94) etc., then there must also be a multiplicity and a diversity of principles, (95) the reply is (96) that although the contraries may go by many names and be of many kinds, yet they are all subsumed under two names, (97) and these two names which are (like) a seed which comprises all the rest, are good and evil. (98) The various names and species (apart from these) are (only) branches[1] (deriving) from these two seeds; (99) and nothing exists that is not included in these two names. (100) There never has been anything nor will there be anything which is neither good nor evil nor a mixture of the two. (101) Thus it is abun-

[1]Reading *dēshaa for dashaa.

dantly clear that there are two first principles, not more, (102) and that good cannot arise from evil nor evil from good.

(103) From this we must infer (104) that what is perfect and complete in its goodness cannot produce evil. (105) If it could, then it would not be perfect, (106) for when a thing is described as perfect, there is no room for anything else (in it); (107) and if there is no room for anything else, nothing else can proceed from it. (108) If God is perfect in goodness and knowledge, plainly ignorance and evil cannot proceed from Him; (109) or if it can, then he is not perfect; (110) and if he is not perfect, then he should not be worshipped as God or as perfectly good.

(111) If (on the other hand) both good and evil originate in God, then he is imperfect so far as goodness is concerned. (112) If he is imperfect in respect of goodness, then he is imperfect in respect of right knowledge. (113) And if he is imperfect in respect of right knowledge, then he is imperfect in respect of reason, consciousness, knowledge, wit, and in all the faculties of knowing. (114) And if he is imperfect in reason, consciousness, wit, and knowledge, he must be imperfect in respect of health; (115) and if he is imperfect in respect of health, he must be sick; (116) and if he must be sick, then he is imperfect in respect of life.

(117) Should it be objected that a single substance like man is seen to originate both good and evil actions, (118) the reason is that man is not perfect in any single respect; (119) and because he is not perfect in respect of goodness, he gives rise to evil. (120) (So too) because he is not perfect in respect of health, he is subject to sickness, (121) and for the same reason he dies: (122) for the cause of death is the conflict of two contrary accidents in one substance, (123) and where there are two contrary acci-

dents in one substance, there are sickness and death to be observed.

(124) Should it be objected that good and bad actions have no (real) existence until they are (actually) performed, (125) the reply is (126) that it is no more possible for an action to exist without an agent than it is for an accident to exist without a substance in which it can inhere; (127) for it is an acknowledged fact that it cannot exist in its own essence or by its own devising. (128) So when a man is angry, Vahuman (the Good Mind) is far from him, (129) and when Vahuman is present within him, anger is not; (130) and when a man tells a lie, truth is far from him, (131) and when he speaks the truth, falsehood has no place in him and such a man is called truthful. (132) Similarly when sickness attacks (a man), health is not in him; (133) and when health supervenes, sickness departs, (134) for a substance cannot change (lit. "move"), but there can be no movement except in a substance.'

CHAPTER V

MAN'S FIRST PARENTS

WE must now leave the rationalist and philosophic climate of Mardān-Farrakh's *Shikand Gumānī Vazār* and his justification of dualism as the only system which adequately accounts for the problem of evil and the creation of the world which must otherwise remain a mystery. In this chapter we must consider what happens to the world after its corruption by the powers of evil. In previous chapters we have had an opportunity of contemplating the two Spirits as they were in the beginning; we have seen how the Evil One initiated hostilities on the intellectual and spiritual plane and how he was hurled back by the utterance of Truth. We have seen how Ohrmazd profited by his discomfiture and how he created both an ideal and a material creation to be a bulwark against the Aggressor when he returned to the assault; and we have seen how this act of creation was forced on the deity as a measure of self-defence, and how the material creation which is bounded by the sky acts as a snare in which Ahriman kicks and struggles like a trapped beast, for he is 'without knowledge, without method.'[1] Finally we witnessed Ahriman's attack on the material creation, his introduction into a perfect world of death and disease, poison and noxious beasts, lust, anger, envy, concupiscence, and all their attendant vices, and last of all his destruction of Gayōmart, the Blessed Man, at the instigation and with the assistance of that

[1] ZZZ, p. 315, §23.

strange figure, the Whore, who seems to be nothing other than the Eternal Feminine in its evil aspect.

The passage we have selected as the text for our present chapter forms the beginning part of the fourteenth chapter of the *Greater Bundahishn* which is entitled 'On the nature of Man.' It is not edifying. The chapter also appears in the shorter or 'Indian' version of the *Bundahishn* and I have followed the text of the latter in many instances.

Gayōmart, as we have seen, is the first father of the human race. He is the First Man in that all human beings proceed from him, but he is himself semi-divine, being the son of Ohrmazd and Spandarmat, the Earth[1]; and in shape he is round and 'shining like the Sun.'[2] He is the First Man in that he is the prototype of man, but he is not the first man in the strict sense of being the first recognizably human being with arms and legs and other distinctively human features. He resembles much more those primitive beings described in Plato's *Symposium*[3] who were spherical in shape and androgynous in sex. The text we have translated in this chapter tells us of the first man proper, Mashyē (or Mahrē) and his sister Mashyānē (or Mahrānē), how they came into being, what they did, and how they fell from grace.

Thirty years after Ahriman invaded the material cosmos Gayōmart died, but in dying, he prophesied, 'Now that the Aggressor has come, men will arise from my seed, and it is best for them to do good works.'[4] God's plan was not to be defeated and 'the Blessed Man' was to live on in the human race; Man, God's masterpiece, was to fight in the front line against the Aggressor held prisoner in the sky.

In our third chapter we saw that there almost certainly

[1]See above, p. 21, §2.   [3]189Dff.
[2]Above, p. 40, §27.   [4]Above, p. 48, §11.

existed a myth in which the 'Blessed Man,' Gayōmart was, as it were, forced into union with Ahriman's consort, the Primal Whore, who can scarcely be anything but the feminine principle just as Gayōmart himself is the male principle. But whereas there is no ambiguity about the male principle, there is considerable ambiguity about the female. Gayōmart himself is said to have sprung from Spandarmat, the Earth, and the seed from which he grows was planted by Ohrmazd himself, Spandarmat's own father.[1] Spandarmat is, as daughter and wife of Ohrmazd, 'the Queen of Heaven and Mother of Creation'[2] : she is, basically, Mother Earth. So in the text we are analysing we find that the seed of the dying Gayōmart falls into his mother, the Earth, and in due course the first human couple, Mashyē and Mashyānē, arise from her in the form of a rhubarb plant. The female principle, then, appears both as the terrible 'Whore' who lets loose 'so much affliction on the Blessed Man and the toiling Bull . . . that they will not be fit to live,'[3] and as the good mother, the gentle Spandarmat whose very name means 'bounteous harmony or devotion.' The Whore, then, is simply the terrible aspect of the female principle just as the Good Mother, Spandarmat, the Earth, is its kindly and beneficent aspect. Spandarmat is what Professor C. G. Jung and his school call the Great Mother, the Whore is the 'Terrible Mother.' They are aspects of one and the same principle, the eternal female, just as Ohrmazd and Ahriman are the two aspects of the eternal male,—in Zoroastrianism eternally divided and in no wise to be reconciled. The apparent confusion, then, introduced by the myth of the Whore is simply due to the division of the female principle into an Ohrmazdean and an Ahrimanian half. Thus

[1]See ZZZ, pp. 367, §36, and 152.   [3]Above, p. 45.
[2]Ibid., p. 152.

it is natural that, beside the myth of Gayōmart's union in death with the Earth Goddess, we find traces of an involuntary union with an impure female fiend which results in his death. She too, presumably, is an aspect of the Earth Goddess, and this goes far to explain how it is possible for Mashyē and Mashyānē, the children of the 'Blessed Man' and Good Mother Earth, to behave in the reprehensible manner described later on in this chapter.

To resume our story. The two of them grew up from the earth in the form of a single and undifferentiated rhubarb stalk. Later they separated and assumed a fully human form.

The position of Mashyē and Mashyānē in a world that has now tasted evil is analogous to that of Adam and Eve when they were expelled from the garden. Admittedly by this time the powers of evil have been brought under some sort of control, and Mashyē and Mashyānē no longer have to stand the full brunt of Ahriman's attack as was the case of the hapless Gayō-mart. The moment they become self-conscious they are sternly admonished by Ohrmazd to do only what is good and on no account to worship the demons. So, dutifully, they acknowledge Ohrmazd as Creator, but no sooner is temptation put in their way than they proclaim Ahriman creator of water, the earth, and plants,—beings, signi-ficantly enough in view of what has been said, regarded by the Zoroastrians as being of the female sex.[1] For this, according to the standards of orthodoxy, appalling blas-phemy 'both were damned; and their souls (shall remain) in Hell till the Final Body.'

Now it is not clear whether Mashyē and Mashyānē were intended to live on earth without taking food. According to Zoroastrian orthodoxy this seems unlikely though it is possible that the more ascetic wing of the

[1] See ZZZ, p. 75.

70

Zoroastrian Church thought otherwise.[1] Be that as it may, they remained for thirty days without taking nourishment of any kind. Only then did they venture to try a little goat's milk, but after drinking it they complained that they felt ill. 'This was their second lie; and the demons obtained strength (thereby)' (§7). Now, in Zoroastrian parlance 'lying' means sinning, and it is therefore implied that either the drinking of the milk was sinful or the feeling of nausea that followed it. Here again there is a certain ambivalence, for the text would naturally be interpreted by the orthodox as meaning that they were condemned for their ingratitude, but by the more ascetically minded heterodox as indicating that they never should have eaten at all, just as in the last days the human race gives up eating and drinking altogether.[2]

Their next physical action is again capable of two interpretations. They slew an animal (either an ox or a sheep, for the word *gōspand* is ambiguous in Pahlavī) and roasted it on a fire which they had made 'on a sign from the spiritual gods.' With the skin of the animal they clothed themselves and with its hair they made rugs thereby learning the art of weaving; they further learnt how to make weapons out of iron and how to carve woodwork with them. They were, in fact, becoming rational and civilized human beings, yet once again are they upbraided. 'Through the ingratitude that they had shown the demons became emboldened' (§11).

What wrong had they done? Plainly the lighting of the fire which they had done at the instigation of the gods cannot have been wrong, nor can the making of clothes from animal hair nor yet the making of implements. In what, then, did their ingratitude consist? Presumably in the slaughter of an innocent beast, in the consumption of its flesh, and in the offering of the sacri-

[1]*Ibid.*, p. 178.   [2]See below, p. 145, and ZZZ, p. 352.

ficial meat to the fire and to the gods on high. If the gift were acceptable, it would scarcely have been intercepted by a vulture as in fact it was. Similarly the first flesh to be consumed on earth was consumed by a dog,—an indication, perhaps, that God did not mean man to be carnivorous.

We shall be dealing very briefly with the question of animal sacrifice in a later chapter. Suffice it to say here that the practice was vigorously attacked by Zoroaster himself, but that it was subsequently admitted in the later Avesta where whole holocausts are mentioned. Throughout the Sassanian period there seems to have been no agreement between the authorities as to whether such sacrifices were admissible or not. Ādhurbādh, son of Mahraspand, however, whom the Pahlavī books regard as *the* great orthodox teacher, bid the faithful 'abstain from the unjust slaughter of oxen and sheep,'[1] but there are many instances of kings and princes offering hecatombs of victims.

What is, however, interesting in this initial sacrifice performed by Mashyē is that it corresponds closely to the sacrifice portrayed on the Mithraic monuments. The presence of a bird,—in this case a vulture, on the monuments a raven,—and the dog in both cases is interesting : for in the Mithraic representations it is the dog which laps up the blood of the slaughtered bull, and the bird which stands between Mithras and the Sun, just as in our text the vulture intercepts the portion of the sacrifice destined for the gods and the dog apparently consumes the portion destined for the fire. This, then, would represent an ancient pre-Zoroastrian form of sacrifice which later became incorporated into Zoroastrianism itself but which later still was again abrogated, being only symbolically offered in bloodless form as it is to this day. In

[1] *Dēnkart* (ed. Madan) p. 217, l.15 ; cf. below, p. 128.

Mithraism, it may be assumed, the sacrifice surv
intact. How Mithra-Mithras came to be associated wɩ
this sacrifice is here irrelevant.[1]

However we choose to interpret the sacrifice offered
by Mashyē and Mashyānē, the fact remains that the
demons were emboldened, and that our first parents
attacked each other savagely, disputing, one may assume,
over the distribution of their new-found treasures. Yield-
ing to temptation again, they now made an offering of
milk to the demons, a gesture which greatly increased
the latter's strength.

Thus Mashyē and Mashyānē proved themselves singularly inept in carrying out their pre-ordained role in
Ohrmazd's plan. Unlike Gayōmart who was himself
sinless, his son and daughter had blasphemed against
their Creator, and as if that were not enough, had sought
to propitiate his deadly enemies by offering them sacrifice. So heinous was this sin and so greatly were the
demons strengthened by it that they were able to make
this stiff-necked couple sexually impotent for fifty years.

We saw in our first chapter what great stress the
Zoroastrians laid on the propagation of the species as a
sacred duty. That the first couple should remain child-
less for fifty years, then, shows how grievously they had
failed in fulfilling the divine purpose. When finally they
produced a pair of twins, they once again did a monstrous thing. 'So sweet were the children that the mother
devoured the one and the father the other. Then
Ohrmazd took away the sweetness of children from them
so that they might rear them and that their children
might survive'! (§14).

The legend of Mashyē and Mashyānē is told in other
sources too, and does not vary much. It is the Zoro-

---

[1] I cannot agree with Hartmann's identification of Mithra with
Mashyē (see his *Gayōmart*, pp. 65ff.).

astrian version of the Fall. Gayōmart is man's prototype and perfect exemplar : he does not fall in any theological sense, he is simply overpowered by overwhelming force and dies. Mashyē and Mashyānē, on the other hand, fall repeatedly ; they blaspheme, they worship the demons, and they devour their own children. Their basic corruption does not seem to be explicable if they are regarded as the children of Gayōmart and Spandarmat, the Earth, as the text clearly states. The story is only comprehensible if we regard them as having sprung from Gayōmart, the 'Blessed Man,' on the one hand, and from the 'Whore,' the evil side of the feminine principle, on the other. Only so can their innate perversity be explained.

Their fall shows that human nature is already basically corrupt, and the power of the demons which they did so much to augment can only be curbed by the bringing of the Good Religion by the Prophet, Zoroaster. Thus the Zoroastrianism of Sassanian times regards the history of the material cosmos as a perpetual looking forward to the *frashkart* or final Rehabilitation at the end of time. The first onslaught is the worst, and the gods themselves have to intervene to retrieve the situation. Mashyē and Mashyānē then make a lamentable beginning and Ohrmazd has to reduce the natural pleasure they take in their food so monstrously excessive does it prove to be. With the establishment of the Good Religion with its doctrine of moderation in all things the worst excesses of the demons of concupiscence are held at bay until the time is ripe for all things to be made new and for the final counter-offensive against Ahriman which destroys his power for ever.

'(1) (Ohrmazd) says in the Religion, "I created man in ten species. First was he who is bright and white-eyed, even Gayōmart. Of the ten species one is Gayōmart, and the (other) nine[1] proceeded from him. The tenth is the monkey, the lowest of men." He says (further), " When Gayōmart was assailed with sickness, he fell on his left side. From his head lead came forth, from his blood zinc, from his marrow silver, from his feet iron, from his bones brass, from his fat crystal, from his arms steel, and from his soul (*jān*) as it departed, gold which even to-day men will only give up with their very life on account of its great value. Because of that portion of death which entered into the body of Gayōmart death will come upon all (living) creatures until the final Rehabilitation."

(2) When Gayōmart passed away and let fall his seed, that seed was purified by the light of the Sun : two parts of it were preserved by Nēryōsang[2] and one part was received by Spandarmat, (the Earth). For forty years it remained in the earth. When the forty years had elapsed, Mashyē and Mashyānē grew out of the earth in the form of a rhubarb plant : one stalk it had and fifteen sprouts. It was as if their hands were clapped to their ears, and they were joined the one to the other, joined in limb and form,[3] and over the two hovered their *khwarr*.[4] So closely

---

[1]Reading *9 for 9-om.
[2]A deity who acts as messenger to the gods.
[3]Reading *ham-dēsak.
[4]This complex idea I have elsewhere rendered as 'dignity.' Here it means 'essence' or 'final cause' which is under the direction of the *ruvān* or rational soul. The *khwarr* of man in the Pahlavī texts is his pre-existent soul as well as his 'final cause' in the Aristotelian sense.

were they linked together that it was not clear which was the male and which the female. The *khwarr* which had been created by Ohrmazd and which accompanied them and is the *khwarr* (soul and dignity) of mankind, was given to them.

(3) For it is said (in the Religion), "Which did (Ohrmazd) create first, the *khwarr* or the body?" And Ohrmazd said, "The *khwarr* was created first and the body afterwards." (The *khwarr*) was put into the body of him for whom it was created, for man's function[1] was fashioned (first) and the body was created for the function. The interpretation of this is that the soul (*ruvān*) was created first, then the body. The soul directs the function within the body.

(4) Then the two of them, (Mashyē and Mashyānē,) developed from plant form into human form, and the *khwarr* which is their soul entered into them secretly (*mēnōkīhā*). Even to-day do trees grow up in this wise,— trees whose fruit is the ten species of man (*sic*).

(5) Ohrmazd said to Mashyē and Mashyānē: "Ye are men, the father (and mother) of the world : do ye your works in accordance with righteous order (*dātastān*) and a perfect mind. Think, speak, and do what is good. Do not worship the demons." Thus did the twain first think when each considered the other, "He is a human being." The first deed that they performed was that they moved and blinked their eyes. And the first thing they said was this: "Ohrmazd created water, the earth, plants, cattle, the stars, the Moon and the Sun, and all fertile things" which in the righteous revelation are called root and fruit.

(6) Then the Aggressor assailed their mind and corrupted it; and they cried out : "The Destructive Spirit created water, the earth, plants, and other things." When

[1] *khwēshkārīh* 'function' ; elsewhere glosses *khwarr* ; cf. ZZZ, p. 173.

they pronounced this first lie which ruined them, they spoke in accordance with the will of the demons. This first joy did the Destructive Spirit (steal) from them (and) make his own. For this lie both were damned; and their souls (shall remain) in Hell till the Final Body.

(7) For thirty days they refrained from food and clothed themselves in grass. After thirty days in the wilderness they came upon a white haired goat and they sucked the milk of its udders. And when they had drunk the milk, Mashyē said to Mashyānē: "I had greater joy when I had not drunk the milk than I have now when I have drunk it : my body is ill." This was their second lie ; and the demons obtained strength (thereby).

(8) And the sweet taste of food was taken from them so that only one hundredth part of it remained.

(9) And after thirty more days and nights (had passed) they came upon a head of cattle, orange (in colour), with white jaws, and they slew it; and on a sign from the spiritual gods they built a fire from the wood of the lote and box, for these two trees are the most productive of fire. And they made the fire to blaze with (the breath of) their mouths, and the first fuel they burnt upon it was straw and *olive and stems of mastic and branches of the date-palm. And they roast the beast on a spit and left a quantity of meat (equal to) three handfuls in the fire saying : "(This is) the portion of the fire." And they threw another portion towards the sky, saying : "This is the portion of the gods." And a vulture passed above them and carried it off from them : for (*sic*) the first flesh (to be consumed) was consumed by the dog.

(10) Next they clothed themselves in garments made of skins. Then they wove a rug[1] in the desert and made woven cloth with which to clothe themselves. And they

[1]Reading *gilīmak*.

fixed a stone[1] in the earth and smelted iron and beat out the iron[2] on the stone and made a knife of it; and with this they cut wood and made a wooden dish.

(11) Through the ingratitude that they had shown the demons became emboldened. And of their own accord (Mashyē and Mashyānē) became wickedly jealous of each other, attacked each other, struck and rent each other and ripped out each other's hair.

(12) Then the demons cried out from the darkness (saying): "Ye are men: worship the demons that your envy may subside." And Mashyānē arose and milked the milk of a cow and poured it out to the Northern quarter.[3] Through the worship that was thus offered to them the demons waxed mightily.

(13) And (Mashyē and Mashyānē's) sexual parts became so dried up that for fifty years they had no desire to have intercourse with each other; and had they had intercourse together, no offspring would have been born to them. And at the end of (these) fifty years they began to think of begetting offspring, first Mashyē and then Mashyānē. For Mashyē said to Mashyānē, *"Mihi ventrum tuum aspicienti exsurgit membrum."* Then Mashyānē said, "Brother Mashyē, *Mihi membrum tuum ingens exsurgens aspicienti palpitat ventrum."* Then they consummated their desires, and in the act of fulfilling their desire they thought: "During the last fifty years this is the deed we should have done."

(14) After nine months a pair of twins was born to them, a girl and a boy. So sweet were the children that the mother devoured the one and the father the other. Then Ohrmazd took away the sweetness of children from them so that they might rear them and that their

---

[1]'Indian' has *D'L*; 'Greater' has *'sag* for *sig* 'stone.' See ZZZ, p. 309. [2]Reading *pat sang *ān āsēn* zat.*
[3]The demons are said to inhabit the North.

children might survive.[1] Seven pairs of twins were born to them, male and female. Each brother took his sister to wife and all six couples stayed with Mashyē and Mashyānē; and from each was born offspring after fifty years, and in a hundred years they all died.'

[1] I follow the 'Indian' version here.

CHAPTER VI

THE GOOD RELIGION

'IN the beginning was the Word : and the Word was
with God : and the Word was God. The same was in the
beginning with God. All things were made by him : and
without him was made nothing that was made. In him
was life : and the life was the light of men. . . . And the
Word was made flesh, and dwelt among us (and we saw
his glory, the glory as it were of the only begotten of
the Father), full of grace and truth.' So does St. John
describe the Second Person of the Holy Trinity and His
incarnation in the person of Jesus Christ.

The doctrine of the Word of God which is at the same
time His Wisdom and His Reason is, of course, not
peculiar to Christianity. What makes Christianity unique
is not the doctrine of the Eternal Word but the incarnation of that Word in a human being.

Islam too has its doctrine of the Word of God and of
the irruption of that Word into the temporal and created
world. But whereas in Christianity the Word becomes
incarnate in the person of Jesus Christ so that Christ,
not the Bible, is by right and nature the prime object of
devotion to the Christian, in Islam the Eternal Word
breaks into time not as the Prophet Muhammad, but as
the Koran which, for Moslems, is the eternal and con-
substantial Word of God. The Prophet Muhammad is
merely the vehicle through which the Word is transmitted to man. If, then, the Christians believe in the
Word made flesh, the Muhammadans believe equally in

the Word made Book. We must now consider whether the Zoroastrians had any such doctrine, and, if so, what they believed the Word to be in this material and temporal world.

We have already seen that 'omniscience and goodness' make up the permanent disposition of Ohrmazd and that these were also called 'the Religion.' 'The interpretation of both is the same, namely the permanent disposition of Infinite Time, for Ohrmazd and the Space, Religion, and Time of Ohrmazd were and are and evermore shall be.'[1] Thus God's omniscience which is identified with 'the Religion,' that is the Zoroastrian religion, seems to be the Zoroastrian version of the doctrine of the Logos or Word. This Religion is itself the very Wisdom of God, his thought through which he creates. Thus in the book of the *Menōk i Khrat* or 'Spirit of Wisdom' we find Wisdom saying: 'From the first among spiritual and material beings was I who am Innate Wisdom with Ohrmazd. And the Creator Ohrmazd fashioned and created, maintains and orders (all) spiritual and material creatures, the gods and all the rest of creation through the power and valour, wisdom and experience of Innate Wisdom. And at the end of the Rehabilitation he will destroy and smite Ahriman and his abortions chiefly by the power of Wisdom. And Sōshyans and Kay-Khusraw and all the others who bring about the Resurrection and the Final Body, will bring it about chiefly by the power and help of Wisdom.

'(All) knowledge and experience on earth, education, and the learning of all trades, and every occupation practised by men in this temporal world, are by Wisdom. The souls of the blessed escape from Hell and go to Heaven chiefly through the power and protection of Wisdom. And men on earth should seek a good life and

[1] Above, p. 35.

81

happiness and a good name and all good things through the power of Wisdom.'[1]

Similarly it is through Wisdom that the embryo is safely preserved in the womb, that the plants grow and the world is full of good things, that the Sun, Moon, and stars follow their appointed courses, that the rains rain, and finally that Man recognizes the truth of the Good Religion. Wisdom, then, is God's Word which gives the world its being and which maintains it in existence; and this Word is identical with the *Dēn,* the Religion.

As the creative Word of God the Religion is summed up in the *Ahunvar* prayer, which, as we have seen, Ohrmazd pronounces at the very beginning of creation and which has the effect of precipitating Ahriman back into his own kingdom of darkness for three thousand years. By pronouncing his Eternal Word God reveals to his Enemy his final defeat and destruction, the creation of the world and its final rehabilitation at the end of time. Ohrmazd's first pronouncement of the *Ahunvar* is the first manifestation of the godhead: it sets the whole creative process in motion and marks the beginning of finite Time. Creation, indeed, is the 'manifestation' of God's eternal Wisdom in the Religion and of his temporal infinity beyond finite Time.

Substantially God's Wisdom and his Religion are one.[2] The Religion is both the unmanifest Wisdom of God, its manifestation in the *Ahunvar* prayer at the beginning of time, and finally, in the form of the Avesta, its full and detailed formulation which the Zoroastrians believe was transmitted by God to Zoroaster. In an interesting passage which Fr. J. de Menasce has recently brought to light,[3] Ohrmazd says, 'I, the Religion, and the Word (exist eternally). The Religion is the act of Ohrmazd;

---

[1] *Mēnōk i Khrat,* Anklesaria, 56. 2–10.   [2] See ZZZ, pp. 207–8.
[3] In *Donum natalicum in H. S. Nyberg oblatum,* p. 51.

82

the Word is his faith. . . . The Religion is superior to the Word because the act is superior to speech.' The passage, though the exact sense is uncertain, seems to imply that the Religion is a larger concept than the word (by which is meant the *Ahunvar*) and that it has eternal as well as temporal existence. The Avesta, then, as being the Religion manifested on earth, is the earthly copy of the divine and eternal exemplar in Heaven : it is the divine Wisdom 'manifested' to Zoroaster on earth.

Zoroaster himself is a prophet and no more than a prophet. Like Muhammad he is simply the vehicle through which the divine Word is transmitted to man. The 'Good Religion,' however, of which he was the vehicle, is not quite identical with the Avesta : it is not so much a book, it is rather a principle. It can be summed up in the following words,—order, righteousness or justice, and the Mean. For the later Zoroastrians the sum of wisdom was the Aristotelian 'Mean.' So wholly did they accept this Greek idea that they claimed it as being specifically Iranian. 'Iran has always commended the Mean,' we are informed,[1] 'and censured excess and deficiency. In the Byzantine Empire the philosophers, in India the learned, and elsewhere the specialists have in general commended the man whose argument showed subtlety, but the kingdom of Iran has shown approval of the (truly) wise.'

The Zoroastrians, then, adopted and enthusiastically proclaimed Aristotle's famous doctrine of the Mean (as indeed they did the equally typically Aristotelian doctrines of matter and form, and potentiality and actuality); and the whole of their ethics in the late Sassanian period is based on this doctrine which sees in virtue a mean between the two extremes of excess and deficiency, between the 'opposite' (*hamēstār*) and the 'kindred' or

[1] *Dēnkart,* ed. Madan, p. 429, l. 11 ; cf. ZZZ, p. 252.

'related' (*brātarōt*) vice. The essence then of the Zoro-astrian ethic is 'nothing in excess' : it is essentially a gentleman's ethical code, a code of moderation and good manners. Opposition to the 'Lie' means opposition to the two extremes of excess and deficiency which are in turn two aspects of *varan,* a term which may mean either concupiscence or heresy. In the theological texts, extracts from which we reproduce in this chapter, *varan* is used exclusively in the sense of heresy, the opposite of *Dēn,* the Religion, and we have so translated it. Character-istic of *varan* or heresy is that it ascribes evil, directly or indirectly, to the supreme God. The term, then, does not only cover the Zoroastrian heresies such as the Zervanite which placed the principle of Infinite Time above Ohrmazd and Ahriman, and indeed made him their father, but also the non-Zoroastrian religions, and par-ticularly Christianity and Islam,—religions which, in Zoroastrian eyes, imputed evil to God. Such a god, they say, is no god at all, he is a demon, and his worshippers are therefore classed among the 'worshippers of the demons,' a term that originally applied only to the wor-shippers of the old Aryan gods whom Zoroaster had dethroned.

The Good Religion, then, is God's Word made mani-fest on earth : all other religions derive from *varan* 'heresy' 'the original word' of which 'is that evil comes from the Creator' (p. 94). The Good Religion is the golden mean between excess and deficiency ; the other religions all derive from these two and are therefore, each in its own way, distortions of the truth which is the Zoroastrian *via media.*

Our first extract in this chapter compares the Good Religion to a tree : its trunk is the Mean ; its two great boughs the religious commands and prohibitions (action and abstention), its three branches the famous triad of good thoughts, good words, and good deeds, its four off-branches the four castes, and its five roots the five degrees of government. Over all stands the King of Kings, 'the Governor of the whole world.'

This brings us to another aspect of the Good Religion. It is the most perfect example of Erastianism to be found on the face of the globe. Church and State are mutually interdependent, and the symbol and crown of both is the King of Kings, the Sassanian monarch who is the guardian of religion as he is of justice and order. Religion indeed, in the Zoroastrian sense, is almost synonymous with justice and order by which is understood the socially stratified order of the Sassanian Empire exemplified in the four castes of priests, warriors, peasants, and artisans, —with the priesthood standing at the top. 'Know,' Ardashīr I is reported as saying,[1] 'that religion and king-ship are two brothers, and neither can dispense with the other. Religion is the foundation of kingship and king-ship protects religion. For whatever lacks a foundation must perish, and whatever lacks a protector disappears.' When the two are perfectly conjoined in one person, the final Rehabilitation will come to pass, for such a com-bination cannot be resisted by Ahriman and the demons who concentrate all their efforts on separating the two. Thus, according to one of our texts, had Yam (that is, the mythical king Jamshīd) who is here represented as the ideal ruler, agreed to accept the Good Religion as well as kingship, or had Zoroaster been endowed with kingship as well as granted the Religion, the millennium would have set in. Only in the Sōshyans, the promised Saviour who, in the last days, will arise from the seed of Zoroaster, are the two united; and it is he who is destined to restore the world.

The comparatively rapid disappearance of Zoro-

[1]Mas‘ūdī, *Les Prairies d'Or*, Barbier de Meynard, vol. II, p. 162.

astrianism after the Muhammadan conquest has always remained somewhat of a puzzle. There is, however, a very cogent psychological reason for this. The fall of the dynasty and the conquest of Iran by 'worshippers of a demon' meant the final end of the marriage of Church and State; and to the Zoroastrian mind the one could not exist apart from the other. Once the world had been deprived of the Great King, the Religion he protected must necessarily succumb, 'for whatever lacks a protector disappears.' Thus the Zoroastrians could only look forward to the coming of the Sōshyans who, by once again bringing together the Religion and the Crown, would be the architect of a new world in which Iran would once again assume her rightful hegemony.

SHIKAND GUMĀNĪ VAZĀR
chapter I, §§11–30

'. . . The Religion of omniscience (is) like a mighty tree (12) with one trunk, two great boughs, three branches, four off-branches, and five roots.[1] (13) And the one trunk is the Mean, (14) the two great boughs are action and abstention, (15) the three branches are *humat, hūkht,* and *huvarsht,* that is, good thoughts, good words, and good deeds. (16) The four off-branches are the four religious castes by which the Religion and secular life are (both) maintained, (17) the priesthood, the warrior caste, the caste of husbandmen, and the caste of artisans. (18) The five roots are the five (degrees of) government whose names in Religion are *mānpat* (householder), *vīspat* (village headman), *zandpat* (tribal chieftain), *dēhpat* (provincial governor) and the *Zarathrushtōtom* (the highest religious authority and representative of

[1]Reading *rīshaa.

Zoroaster on earth). (19) (Over and above these) is another, the Chief of all chiefs, that is the King of Kings, the governor of the (whole) world.

(20) And in the microcosm[1] which is Man ⟨four things⟩ are seen to correspond to these four earthly castes, (21) the head to priesthood, (22) the hands to the warrior caste, (23) the belly to the caste of husbandmen, (24) and the feet to the caste of artisans. (25) So too the four virtues indwelling Man, that is, temperance, fortitude, reason, and energy. (26) Priesthood corresponds to temperance, for temperance is the highest duty of the priests, for through temperance they do not commit sin for very shame and fear. (27) The warrior caste corresponds to fortitude, for fortitude is the sovereign adornment of the warriors; it is explained (as meaning) "innate manliness." (28) Reason corresponds to the caste of husbandmen, for the function of *reason[2] is the tilling of the soil and the promotion of a continuous evolution towards the final Rehabilitation. (29) Energy corresponds to the caste of artisans, for it is the greatest stimulant of their trade. (30) All these diverse functions (are based) on the one trunk of righteousness (truth) and the Mean (and are) opposed to the Lie and its organs which are their opposites.'

ON INNATE WISDOM
(*Dēnkart*, ed. Madan, pp. 117–19)

'The Good Religion is Innate Wisdom (or reason): and the forms and virtues of Innate Wisdom are of the same stock as Innate Wisdom itself. These forms and virtues are begotten of Vahuman (the Good Mind) and the Bounteous Spirit (Ohrmazd).

[1]Reading *kōdaa* for *kardaa*.   [2]Reading *khardī* for *ardī*.

False religion[1] is ruinous heresy : and the forms and vices of ruinous heresy are of the same vile stock as ruinous heresy itself. These forms and vices of ruinous heresy are misbegotten of Akōman (the Evil Mind) and the Destructive Spirit.

For[2] the original seed of the Good Religion is the Bounteous Spirit, and the original seed of false religion is the Destructive Spirit. The Good Religion is manifested in wisdom, conformity with wisdom, in that which has wisdom for its matter and wisdom for its form, in wise action, in good progress that conforms to wisdom, in light which is analogous to wisdom, and in all the benefit that accrues to the good creations in virtue of its being begotten of the Bounteous Spirit.

False religion is manifested in heresy, conformity with heresy, in that which has heresy for its matter and heresy for its form, in heretical (self-opinionated) action, in evil progress that conforms to heresy, in darkness which is analogous to heresy, and in the universal harm that accrues to the good creations in virtue of its being misbegotten of the Destructive Spirit.

(Now we must speak of) the spheres of influence (ravākīh) of both. In its pure state (i.e. uncontaminated with evil) the sphere of influence of the Good Religion consists in its inhering, by its goodness and purity, ⟨in⟩ the Amahraspands where Innate Wisdom exercises absolute sovereignty, and where ruinous heresy is altogether without jurisdiction. The sphere of influence of false religion is among the demons where ruinous heresy exercises full sovereignty and from where Innate Wisdom is most remote.

In the mixed state (the sphere of influence of) both is in the material world in which Innate Wisdom and

[1] Reading *aghdēn mūtak* for *akōman 'kē*.
[2] Reading *'chē rādh* for *'kē 'nē*.

ruinous heresy struggle for supremacy. In the mixed state the degree in which Innate Wisdom is strong and sovereign corresponds exactly to the degree in which the Good Religion is accepted, believed, and propagated, the gods reign, the good is great, and the temporal world prospers. (So too) the degree in which ruinous heresy is strong and great corresponds exactly to the degree in which false religion is accepted and spread abroad, the demons hold violent sway, evil men are great, and the temporal world declines.

(Now we must speak of) the fruits of these influences. The fruit of the Good Religion is the benefit of creatures, that of false religion is their harm.

The fruit of the benefit (brought) by the Good Religion whose sphere of influence in the pure state is among the Amahraspands, consists in the protection (extended) by them to creatures ⟨against⟩ the disruption caused by the Aggressor, the emanation of the power of their goodness into human nature by guarding the will in purity, by disciplining (*ānītan*) the character, by establishing in man his very humanity which is his salvation and his adornment, by increasing and multiplying virtue in the world, and by ordering the world in goodness.

(The fruits and benefits of the Good Religion) whose[1] sphere of influence in the mixed state is in Man consist in the strengthening of good character and of the virtues in Man, in the overcoming and conquest of the Lie, in the sanctification (*kirpakēnītan*) of (Man's) actions so that his soul may be saved, in its total diffusion throughout the human race, the defeat of the hosts of the Lie, the destruction (and expulsion) of the Aggressor from creation, and the gift of immortality and sovereignty in freedom to all the good creation.

The fruit of the harm of false religion whose evil

[1]Reading *'kē* for *'hach*.

sphere of influence in the pure state is among the demons, consists in their pouring out adversity in order to destroy the material world and to damage creatures. And (the fruit of the harm of false religion) whose sphere of influence in the mixed state is in Man, consists in the strengthening of the vices and weakening of the virtues, in the destruction of Man's very humanity and in sowing devilry in him, in the vitiating of his actions and the damnation of his soul, in doing damage to the earth and in laying it waste by injustice through the corruption of Man's humanity by devilry. Injustice gives strength to the demons in their ruining of the material world. Were evil allowed to run its course, unmixed and wholly unrestrained, and were goodness to be annihilated in the world (completely), it would mean that creation, in such a state of total evil unmixed with goodness, could not exist or endure even for a moment.'[1]

THE ESSENCE OF THE GOOD RELIGION
(*Dēnkart,* ed. Madan, pp. 329–30)

'The essence of the Good Religion is the Wisdom of Ohrmazd, and his Wisdom (consists in) bestowing, knowing, and doing. Its matter is omniscience, righteousness (truth) towards all things, and giving to all things what is proper to them : this is the character of Ohrmazd. Its function is to heal creation. Its operation is summed up in recognizing by knowledge the potentialities that are created in things, and by action in putting them to their proper use.

Its power to act consists in putting the potentialities which are created in things to their proper use, in removing the corruption which is inherent in creatures owing

[1] Reading *nisangchak.*

to their being mixed with the Aggressive Power, and in healing creatures both materially and spiritually. The benefit (derived from) its quantitative knowledge (of particulars) and from its operations in time is its (continuous) forward movement and its control (of the world) for the duration of the millennia (which leads) up to the final Rehabilitation. By recognizing the potentialities that are in things, by putting the whole creation to its full use through action, and by healing it (and saving it) from the Adversary, it attains to the eternal order, perfect, entire, and full of bliss.'

THE RELIGION AS THE MEAN
(*Dēnkart*, ed. Madan, pp. 46-7)

'The Religion of the worshippers of Ohrmazd is Wisdom (*dānākīh*). Its being is from the Mean which is the essence of the Religion and the opposite of which is excess and deficiency. Of the antagonists of Wisdom excess is the related opposite and deficiency the contrary opposite. Because noble and right knowledge belongs to the Good Religion the (qualities) most hospitable to it are chiefly faith and knowledge. All (necessary knowledge) about the being of the Religion of the worshippers of Ohrmazd and about what one who professes that Religion should know in the sphere of thought, word, and deed, and about anything that may not have been codified(?),[1] is revealed through the being and manifestation of the Religion.'

Dēnkart, ed. Madan, p. 295

'The usefulness of all actions and things is through the Mean. They are spoilt and made ineffective by

[1] Reading 'hach-ich ⟨ān i⟩ ōshmurishn 'nē mat 'ēstēt.

excess and deficiency. The Mean is under the control of the Innate Wisdom of the Creator (operating) in his creatures. Lack of order is specifically[1] excess and deficiency, diabolical heresy, the opposite (*pityārak*) of Innate Wisdom. Whenever the divine Innate Wisdom triumphs over diabolical heresy among men, the Mean and order are victorious, excess and deficiency are weakened, and creation prospers. So far as men are concerned the Creator (Ohrmazd) made Innate Wisdom supreme in the King (*dahyupat*) so that he might vanquish heresy, the most violent Lie, thereby, and by munificence backed by physical force and by good government of men might arouse their innate wisdom after it had been extinguished by heresy so that their minds might be open to reasonable advice and that order and the Mean might be spread among them and that creation might be well governed.'

THE RELIGION IN ACTION
(*Dēnkart,* ed. Madan, pp. 306–7)

'The action of the Good Religion of the worshippers of Ohrmazd is summed up in the bringing of the excess and deficiency caused by the Aggressor in creation back to the Mean, and in the salvation and comfort of all creation. And since the Creator Ohrmazd sent the Religion of the worshippers of Ohrmazd for the purpose of vanquishing the Aggressor and of bringing comfort to his creation, and since his will is to vanquish the Aggressor and to perfect his creatures, his total Wisdom, though it (appears as) the individual direction of individual creatures, is summed up in one thing, the all-powerful Mean. The Aggressor, (on the other hand,)

[1] Reading **'nāmchisht* for *'nām-chashmīh*.

disrupts creation by means of two (weapons) which contain the whole power of the Lie,—excess and deficiency, the one being a tendency to go beyond the Mean, the other being a tendency to lag behind it. Both bring death and destruction on the creation of Ohrmazd. When creation is brought back to the Mean in cases where there is excess, or brought forward to the Mean in cases where there is deficiency, then does the Religion of the worshippers of Ohrmazd, in its wisdom, save all things (lit. action) from all evil and bring them back to a total goodness and a perfect equilibrium (*dātīkīh*). So have the ancient sages said when expounding the Good Religion that the Religion of Ohrmazd is one single word, the Mean, and that the religion of Ahriman is two words, excess and deficiency.'

THE FRUITS OF THE RELIGION
(*Dēnkart,* ed. Madan, pp. 251–2)

'The original Word of the Good Religion is that all good comes from the Creator and that no[1] evil comes from him : in this is contained all the good that creatures enjoy from the original creation till the final Rehabilitation. Thus from belief in this original Word of the Good Religion proceeds the formation of character, from the formation of character the Mean : from the Mean is justice born, from justice good thoughts, good words, and good deeds ; from good thoughts, good words, and good deeds the welfare of Man. By the welfare of Man are the gods well pleased and strengthened and the demons distressed and vanquished. When the gods are well pleased and strengthened and the demons distressed and vanquished, the spiritual world is made straight and

[1] Reading *'nē* for *rās*.

the material world brought into order. When the spiritual world is thus made straight and the material world put in order, creation is ripe for the final Rehabilitation and merges into it, the Rehabilitation is brought about and all creation is administered in purity and goodness.

The original word of false religion is that evil comes from the Creator : in this is contained all the evil that creatures suffer from the original creation till the final Rehabilitation. Thus from being beguiled by this original word of false religion proceeds the corruption of character, from corruption of character excess and deficiency, ⟨from⟩ excess and deficiency injustice, ⟨from injustice⟩ evil thoughts, evil words, and evil deeds, and from evil thoughts, evil words, and evil deeds, the distress of Man. By the distress of Man are the demons rejoiced and the gods distressed. When the demons are rejoiced and the gods distressed, then are the demons emboldened to upset and disturb the temporal world and to do harm and injury to the material world.'

RELIGION AND KINGSHIP OR CHURCH AND STATE
(*Dēnkart,* ed. Madan, pp. 201–2)

'The Good Religion is the mother of Innate Wisdom and is adorned with Wisdom. Pre-eminently it stores up knowledge of higher things, preserves the mystery of the good spiritual world, ⟨worships⟩ the highest God as God, the Eternal, the All-good, Creator and Preserver. For in conformity with it is praise. Its basis is the nobility inherent in the Iranian (*ērīh*), its matter is the Mean, its essence order (*dātastān*), its home holiness, and its helpmate kingship. Those who profess it form their characters, increase in wisdom, develop their human dignity (*khwarr*) in co-operation with kingship, Religion's helpmate. (Through them) all men hold themselves erect, the times are good, the world prospers, the Aggressor is vanquished, and creation sees salvation. In it (the Religion) is the priesthood, the warrior caste, the caste of husbandmen, and the caste of artisans, the worship of Ohrmazd, increase (*dahmīh*) and (all) other excellencies, virtues, and goodness.

False religion is the mother of heresy and the opponent of wisdom. It stores up false incantations, preserves the dreadful mystery of the evil spiritual world, represents demons in the guise of gods, worships 'Lies' under the names of gods, propagates disorder in the name of order. Excess and deficiency are its matter, deceit its lair, tyranny its helpmate. Those who profess it ruin their own character, overthrow their own reason, diminish their human dignity in co-operation[1] with tyranny, the helpmate of (false religion). Through it are all men beguiled, the times are evil, the world suffers adversity, the Aggressor is strengthened, good creatures are made to reel. In it (false religion) is false priesthood (*ahramōghīh*), tyranny, wolfishness, deception, suffering, worship of the demons, diminution, and (all) other imperfections, sins, and evil.'

Dēnkart, ed. Madan, pp. 129–30

'The thing against which the Destructive Spirit struggles most violently is the coming together in full force of the dignities (*khwarr*) of kingship and the Good Religion in one person, because such a conjunction must destroy him. For if the highest power of the dignity of the Good Religion had been joined to the highest power of the dignity of kingship in Yam,[2] or if the highest power of the dignity ⟨of kingship⟩ as it existed in Yam

[1]Reading *apākīh*.   [2]See p. 85. Text has *ham* for *yam*.

95

had been joined to the highest power of the dignity of the Good Religion in Zoroaster, then the Destructive Spirit would have met with swift destruction, creation would have escaped from the Aggressor, and the desired Rehabilitation would have been brought about in the (two) worlds. (For) whenever in this world piety is linked with good rule in one single pious and good ruler, then is vice weakened and virtue increased, opposition diminishes and co-operation augments, there is more of holiness and less of wickedness among men, the good prosper and prevail and the wicked are straitened and deprived of sovereignty, the world is prosperous, all creation rejoices, and the common people are well off; and by all these things is the world well ordered and adorned. When these two dignities meet in one man, then will the Aggressor be completely vanquished and creation saved and purged. From this the final Rehabilitation proceeds. The Good Religion reveals that these two dignities will meet together in Sōshyans.'

CHAPTER VII

THE GOOD ETHICS

ZOROASTRIANISM is predominantly an ethical religion. This follows naturally from its theological premises, or perhaps it would be more true to say that the theological premises are based on an essentially moralistic view of life. For the Zoroastrian, as we have seen, the prime and inescapable fact of life is evil. Good is good, and evil evil, and it is impossible for the one to proceed from the other. To deny the existence of a separate principle of evil is tantamount to imputing evil to God. This is unthinkable : therefore evil must be a separate principle. Thus Zoroastrian morality is expressed in the three words, *humat, hūkht,* and *huvarsht,*—good thoughts, good words, and good deeds, and the greatest of these is good deeds.

In this chapter we reproduce in translation three texts. The first two are attributed to Ādhurbādh, son of Mahraspand, a character about whom we will have to say a few words, while the third is taken from the *Mēnōk i Khrat,* '(The Book) of the Spirit of Wisdom,' an imaginary dialogue in the form of a catechism in which the Spirit of Wisdom is represented as replying to a series of questions put by a 'wise man.' I have selected the two texts attributed to Ādhurbādh because he was generally regarded as being the final exponent of Zoroastrian orthodoxy in Sassanian times. The Pahlavi books that have survived treat him as the very canon of orthodoxy and the *Dēnkart* claims authority for its teaching by tracing it back to him.

Ādhurbādh lived in the reign of Shāpūr II (A.D. 309–79) at a time, it would appear, when Zoroastrian orthodoxy was still ill-defined. His principal opponents appear to have been the fatalists,[1] a Zervanite sect which made Fate or Time an independent principle against which Man was powerless. This sect, then, denied the basic Zoroastrian doctrine of the freedom of the human will and thereby destroyed the whole basis of Zoroastrian dualism. To confute this and other sects Ādhurbādh volunteered to submit to ordeal by molten brass. The metal was poured on to his chest but he emerged from the ordeal unhurt. This miraculous event was held to prove that Ādhurbādh's views were alone orthodox and they were so proclaimed by the Great King. 'After Ādhurbādh had been vindicated by the consistency of his views, (the King) issued a declaration before all those representatives of the different sects, doctrines, and schools in this wise, "Now that we have seen the Religion upon earth, we shall not tolerate false religions and we shall be exceeding zealous." And thus did he do.'[2]

The two first texts of this chapter are both attributed to this man, and though they may well not be genuine, they do, in all probability, faithfully represent the great man's views. However that may be, they have been included because the very name of Ādhurbādh guarantees their orthodoxy and because they are quintessentially Zoroastrian.

We saw in our last chapter that the Religion came to be equated with the Mean. So too, in these ethical texts, we find that the keynote is moderation. This is the morality of an aristocratic and urbane society. Here no counsels of perfection are to be found, no extremes of self-sacrifice, no commands to love one's enemy or to turn the other cheek. For Ādhurbādh there is no question

[1] *Shikand Gumānī Vazār*, 10. 71.   [2] See ZZZ, p. 8.

of loving one's enemy. This would be going too far. All that is required and all that prudence dictates is that one should keep out of his way. It is true that one or two of these sayings attributed to Ādhurbādh have a mildly Christian flavour. 'Put out of your mind what is past and do not fret and worry about what has not yet come to pass' is reminiscent of Christ's command not to take thought for the morrow. Similarly the sayings 'Do not do unto others what would not be good for yourself' and 'wherever you sit at a banquet, do not sit in the highest seat lest you be moved away therefrom and made to sit in a lower seat' are both closely parallelled in the New Testament. There is, however, no reason to think that there was any direct borrowing since parallels can easily be found elsewhere, for instance in the Buddhist scriptures.

The whole tone and flavour of Ādhurbādh's sayings, however, is wholly unlike that of Christ. The emphasis is always on moderation and the avoidance of extremes. What is demanded first and foremost of man, we might almost say, is common sense. Indeed, the word *khrat* which, in these texts, I have translated as 'wisdom' though elsewhere 'reason' seems to be nearer the true meaning, might be better translated as 'common sense'; and the commonsense view of life is that a man should enjoy the good things of this world while at the same time preparing himself, by right and reasonable conduct, for eternal life in Heaven. Asceticism on the one hand and pure hedonism on the other are extremes and therefore to be avoided. If anything, the former is the worse of the two for it implies an insult to God who made the world and made it good, and who put Man into it to combat evil which can only be achieved by making the world to prosper.

Ādhurbādh's views on how one should occupy oneself

on the different days of the month are particularly pleasing; the emphasis is always on keeping oneself usefully employed and on enjoyment. The tone is set by the prescription for the first day of the month, 'On the day of Ohrmazd drink wine and make merry.' Life on this world is, for the Zoroastrian, not an exile in a valley of tears but a thoroughly satisfactory and enjoyable condition. Perhaps the most striking illustration of this is Ādhurbādh's recommendations for the day dedicated to Rashn, the god whose function it is to judge the soul at death. On such a day, one might have thought, a man might well occupy himself with thoughts of the dreadful reckoning. Far from it. 'On the day of Rashn,' says Ādhurbādh, 'life is gay: do, in holiness, anything you will.' What admirable advice!

Yet though Ādhurbādh recommends a reasonable indulgence in the good things of this life, he has no exaggerated expectations from his fellow-men and none at all from women. 'Men,' he says, 'are like a water-skin full of air. When it is deflated nothing remains'; or again they 'are like suckling babes, creatures of habit who cling to their habits.' His views are summed up in his advice to his son, 'Do not put your trust or confidence in anyone or anything at all.' As to women, 'Put not your trust in women lest you have cause to be ashamed and to repent. Do not tell your secrets to women lest (all) your toiling be fruitless.' This is not, perhaps, to take a very high view of human nature; it does, however, show a healthy scepticism.

Truthfulness, generosity, contentment with one's lot, and good breeding are the virtues he desires to inculcate. Of the vices he singles out vengefulness as perhaps the most heinous, though he is equally severe on calumny and slander both of which show bad breeding. It is also refreshing to find in a religious text the beautiful words,

'So far as you possibly can, do not bore your fellow men.'
The words I have translated as 'bore' mean literally
'afflict by speaking,' a perfect definition of our English
word. That Ādhurbādh should regard the bore as being
a positively sinful individual, does credit to his insight,
for of all the forms of selfishness it is the most devastating
as well as being the most obtuse. To a Zoroastrian it is
a sin because it is the height of bad manners, and bad
manners are in themselves sinful.

'Live a good and useful life, be considerate to others,
fulfil your religious duties, cultivate the land, rear a
family and bring up your children to be literate and
cultivated. Remember at the same time that this life is
only a prelude to the next and that your soul will have
to answer for the deeds you did on earth.' This is the
purport of the sayings of Ādhurbādh, son of Mahraspand. It may be objected that this morality is all too
reminiscent of the morality of the better type of British
public school. It is, and it is none the worse for that.

Our last text from the *Mēnōk i Khrat* concerns the
drinking of wine. This is a little gem of urbane wisdom
and I leave the reader to savour it in itself for it needs
neither introduction nor comment.

THE COUNSELS OF ĀDHURBĀDH, SON OF MAHRASPAND
(*Pahlavī Texts*, pp. 58–71)

'(1) It is related that Ādhurbādh had no child of his
body and that he thereafter put his trust in the gods.
And it was not long before a son was (born) to Ādhurbādh, and because Zoroaster, son of Spitām, had an
upright character, he called him Zartusht (Zoroaster),
and said "Arise, my son, that I may teach you civilized
behaviour (*frahang*).

(2) My son, think upon virtue and do not turn your thoughts to sin, for man does not live eternally and the things of the spirit are the more greatly to be desired.

(3) Put out of your mind what is past and do not fret and worry about what has not yet come to pass.

(4) Put not your trust and confidence in kings and princes.

(5) Do not do unto others what would not be good for yourself.

(6) Be single-minded among rulers and friends.

(7) Do not deliver yourself up as a slave to any man.

(8) Stay far away from any man who approaches you in anger or in enmity.

(9) Hope always and everywhere in the gods and make friends with such men as will profit you.

(10) Strive for the things of the gods and of the Amahraspands and lay down your life for them (if need be).

(11) Tell no secret to a woman.

(12) Listen to all that you hear and do not repeat it at random.

(13) Do not let your wife and children (out of your sight) except for reasons of good manners (*frahang*) lest care and grievous annoyance come upon you and you rue it.

(14) Do not give (alms) out of season.

(15) Give an ambiguous answer (only) when this is befitting.

(16) Do not mock at anyone.

(17) Do not share your secrets with a wrong-headed man. (18) Do not make a choleric man your travelling companion. (19) Do not take a frivolous man for your counsellor. (20) Do not make a rich man the companion of your table. (21) Do not make a drunkard your boon-companion. (22) Do not borrow from a man of bad

character or base lineage or lend to him, for you will pay heavily in interest, and he will be forever at your door or will always be sending messengers to your house, and great loss will you suffer thereby. (23) Do not summon an ill-disposed person to help you. (24) Do not show your property to an envious man. (25) Do not put into force(?) a false judgement in the presence of rulers. (26) Do not listen to the words of calumniators and liars. (27) Do not be over-zealous in punishing others. (28) Do not pick a quarrel at a feast. (29) Do not strike others. (30) Do not strive for position.

(31) Consult men who are of gentle stock, experienced in affairs, clever, and of good character; make these your friends. (32) Take great care that no heavy burden is laid on you in battle.[1] (33) Keep away from vengeful men in a position of power.

(34) Do not come into conflict with a scribe. (35) Do not tell your secrets to a babbler.

(36) Hold a wise man whose position is exalted in high esteem, ask his opinion and listen to it.

(37) Do not tell a lie to anyone. (38) Do not accept the goods of any man who is devoid of shame. (39) Do not consciously wager on anything at all. (40) Do not take an oath on either what is true or what is false.

(41) When you are about to set up house, first take stock of the expense. (42) Woo the woman who is to be your wife yourself. (43) If you (already) have property, start by buying more irrigated agricultural land, for even if it fails to yield interest, the capital will remain.

(44) So far as you possibly can, do not bore your fellow men. (45) Do not seek to be avenged on others and do not try to cause them loss. (46) Be as generous with your property as you can. (47) Do not deceive anyone lest you come to grief thereby. (48) Hold your superiors

[1]Translation uncertain.

in high esteem, make much of them, and listen to what they say. (49) Borrow only from relations and. friends. (50) Cherish the woman who is modest and give her in marriage to a clever and knowledgeable man, for clever and knowledgeable men are like the good earth which yields all manner of produce when once the seed has been planted in it.

(51) Be plain in your speech. (52) Never speak without reflection. (53) Lend money only under agreed conditions (*pat adhvēn*). (54) Cherish a wise and modest woman and ask her in marriage. (55) Choose a son-in-law who is good-natured, honest, and experienced even though he be poor, for he will (surely) receive riches from the gods. (56) Do not mock at your elders, for you are subject to them. (57) Do not send a proud and pitiless man to prison, but choose prison-warders from among big men and (set) an intelligent man (over them).

(58) If you have a son, send him to a grammar-school when he is still a boy, for the art of reading and writing is exceedingly well seen. (59) Speak sharply only after much reflection, for there are times when it is better to speak out and times when it is better to hold your peace; (on the whole) to hold one's peace is better than to speak. (60) Choose a man who tells the truth as your messenger. (61) Do not appoint a bought[1] slave above trustworthy and faithful servants. Spend according to your means. (62) Be courteous in your speech. (63) Keep your conversation courteous. (64) Keep your thoughts righteous. (65) Do not praise yourself; only so will you perform righteous deeds. (66) When in the presence of kings and princes do not appear to be without mercy. (67) Ask the advice of good men of mature age. (68) Accept nothing from a thief nor give anything to him : drive him rather away. (69) As you fear Hell, punish

[1]Reading *'khrītak* for *zatak*.

others only after due reflection. (70) Do not put your trust or confidence in anyone or anything at all.

(71) Make good use of authority so that you may obtain a good position (thereby). (72) Be without sin so that you may be without fear. (73) Be grateful so that you may be worthy of good things. (74) Be single-minded so that you may be faithful. (75) Speak the truth so that you may be trusted. (76) Be humble so that you may have many friends. (77) Have many friends so that you may enjoy a good repute. (78) Be of good repute so that you may live at ease. (79) Choose the better part and love your Religion so that you be saved (*ahrov*). (80) Think on the state of your soul so that you may go to Heaven. (81) Be generous so that you may go to Paradise (*garōdhmān*).

(82) Do not seduce other men's wives, for that is a grievous sin for thy soul. (83) Do not maintain mean and ungrateful men, for they will not thank you. (84) Do not destroy your own soul for the sake of anger or vengeance. (85) When you feel an urgent desire to do or say (something), ⟨ask⟩ politely and say a prayer, for no one ever broke his back by saying his prayers or got foul breath by asking politely. (86) Do not address a low-born person first. (87) When you attend a gathering, do not sit next to a wrong-headed man so that you may not yourself appear wrong-headed. (88) Wherever you sit at a banquet, do not sit in the highest seat lest you be moved away therefrom and made to sit in a lower seat. (89) Do not rely on property and the goods of this world, for property and the goods of this world are like a bird that flies from one tree to another and stays on none. (90) Honour your father and mother, listen to them and obey them, for so long as a man's father and mother live, he is like a lion in the jungle which has no fear of anyone at all; but he who has neither father nor mother is like

a widowed woman who is despoiled by men and can do nothing about it and whom all men despise. (91) Give your daughter to a clever and knowledgeable man, for a clever and knowledgeable man is like the good earth which yields up much grain once the seed is sown in it.

(92) If you would not be abused by others, do not abuse anyone. (93) Do not be violent or ill-considered in your speech, for the man who is violent or ill-considered in his speech is like a fire that falls upon a forest and burns up all birds and fish and creeping things. (94) Do not collaborate with a man who ill-treats his father and mother and with whom they are displeased, lest your justice be turned to injustice(?) and you be deprived of friends and have no pleasant intercourse with anyone. (95) Do not out of false modesty or shame deliver your soul up to Hell. (96) Do not say anything that has a double meaning. (97) When you sit in an assembly, do not sit next to a liar lest you yourself should suffer greatly thereby. (98) Take things easy (lit. 'be easy-footed') so that you may be a welcome guest. (99) Rise before dawn so that your work may prosper. (100) Do not make a new friend out of an old enemy, for an old enemy is like a black snake which does not forget old injuries for a hundred years. (101) Renew your friendship with old friends, for an old friend is like old wine which becomes better and more fit for the consumption of princes the older it is. (102) Praise the gods and be glad of heart, for it is from the gods that you will obtain an increase in the good things (of this world). (103) Do not curse a man of princely rank, for there are security officers in (all) the realm who decree what is good for (the king's) subjects.

(104) I say unto you, my son, that[1] in the affairs of men the greatest(?) helper and the best is wisdom, for if one's wealth is scattered and lost or if one's livestock die,

[1]Reading *'ku* for *'kē*.

wisdom remains. (105) Strive to be firmly anchored in your Religion, for contentment is the highest wisdom (*dānākīh*) and the greatest spiritual hope. (106) Keep your soul ever in mind. (107) Do not forsake your duty to preserve your good name. (108) Keep your hands from stealing, your feet from treading the path of undutifulness, and your mind from unlawful desires (*varan*), for whoso practices virtue obtains his reward, and whoso commits sin receives his punishment. (109) Whoso digs a pit for his enemies will fall into it himself.

(110) The good man lives at ease but the bad man suffers distress and grievous woe. (111) Marry a young wife. (112) Drink wine in moderation, for whoso drinks wine immoderately falls into many a sin. (113) Since you know well that a snake has many wiles, do not be overhasty to touch one lest it bite you and you instantly die. (114) Even though you know well a stretch of water much frequented by bathers, do not be over-hasty in going into rough water lest the water carry you away and you instantly die. (115) Do not on any account be false to a contract lest you be held accountable(??) for it. (116) Do not rob others of their property nor keep (what has been robbed) nor add it to your own, for (then) your own (property) will be destroyed and vanish away, for when you carry off property that is not your own and keep it and ⟨add⟩ it to your own ... (gap in text) ...

(117) ... do not rejoice, for men are like a water-skin full of air. When it is deflated, nothing remains. Men are like suckling babes, creatures of habit who cling to their habits.

(Duties to be performed on different days of the month)

(119) On the day of Ohrmazd drink wine and make

merry. (120) On the day of Vahuman put on new clothes. (121) On the day of Artvahisht go to the Fire Temple. (122) On the day of Shahrēvar rejoice. (123) On the day of Spandarmat till your land. (124) On the day of Hurdāt dig your irrigation channels. (125) On the day of Amurdāt plant shrubs and trees. (126) On the day of Dadhv-pat-Ātur wash your head and trim your hair and nails. (127) On the day of Ātur (Fire) go for a walk and do not bake bread for it is a grievous sin. (128) On the day of Āpān (the Waters) abstain from water and do not vex the waters. (129) On the day of Khwar (the Sun) take your children to the grammar-school so that they may become literate and wise. (130) On the day of Māh (the Moon) drink wine and hold converse with your friends and ask a boon of King Moon. (131) On the day of Tīr (Sirius) send your children to learn archery and jousting and horsemanship. (132) On the day of Gōsh (the Bull) see to the stables and train your oxen to the plough. (133) On the day of Dadhv-pat-Mihr wash your head and trim your hair and nails, and (pick) your grapes from the vine and throw them into the wine-press so that they may become good. (134) On the day of Mihr, if you have been wronged by anyone, stand before Mihr (Mithra) and ask justice of him and cry out aloud (to him). (135) On the day of Srōsh ask a boon of the blessed Srōsh for the salvation of your soul. (136) On the day of Rashn life is gay: do, in holiness, anything you will. (137) On the day of Fravartīn take no oath, and on that day sacrifice to the Fravahrs (departed spirits) of the blessed so that they may be the better pleased. (138) On the day of Vahrām lay the foundations of your house so that it may be speedily completed, and go out to battle and warfare so that you may return the victor. (139) On the day of Rām summon your wife and do (with her) what is done and enjoy yourself : take any suit (you may have) before the judges so that you may return victorious or acquitted. (140) On the day of Vāt (the Wind) confine yourself to words(?) and do not undertake anything new. (141) On the day of Dadhv-pat-Dēn do anything you like, bring your wife into your quarters, trim your hair and nails and clothe yourself. (142) On the day of Dēn (the Religion) kill noxious beasts and reptiles. (143) On the day of Art buy any new thing (you need) and bring it home. (144) On the day of Ashtāt deliver over your mares, cows, and pack-animals to their males so that they may return in good health. (145) On the day of Āsmān (the Sky) set out on a long journey so that you may return safely. (146) On the day of Zamdāt (the Earth) do not take medicine. (147) On the day of Mahraspand mend your clothes, stitch them, and put them on, and take your wife to bed so that a keen-witted and goodly child may be born (to you). (148) On the day of Anaghrān (the Endless Light) trim your hair and nails and take your wife to bed so that an exceptional child may be born (to you).

(149) Do not be overjoyed in[1] good times nor over-distressed in bad times, for the good fortune of Time turns ⟨to⟩ misfortune and the misfortune of Time turns to good fortune, and there is no "up" that has not been preceded by a "down," and no "down" that is not followed by an "up," (150) Do not 'be gluttonous (*varanīk*) in eating your food, (151) and do not partake of all foods. Do not be over-hasty to attend the feasts and banquets of the great lest you return from them abashed. (152) For there are four things which are most harmful to the body of (mortal) men and make them have wrong ideas about their body. One is to glory in one's strength. One is the luxury of pride which (leads

[1]Reading *'kadh* for *'chē*.

one) to pick a quarrel with a well-established (*hangat*) man. One is (the case of) the elderly man with a puerile character who weds an adolescent girl; and one is (the case of) the young man who weds an old woman. (153) It should be known that love of one's fellow men (proceeds) from a balanced mind (*bavandak-mēnishnīh*), and good character from being nicely spoken. (154) And I say unto you, my son, that[1] of all the things that give help to man wisdom is the best".'

SOME SAYINGS OF ĀDHURBĀDH, SON OF MAHRASPAND
(*Pahlavī Texts,* pp. 144–53)

'(1) These are some of the sayings of Ādhurbādh, son of Mahraspand, spoken by him on his death-bed to the people. He taught them (on these lines): "Remember (what I say now) most particularly (*pat dakhshak*) and act accordingly. Do not hoard against the day when you may be in need, for what you hoard . . . [2] except to . . . want does not come sparingly. (2) Strive to hoard up only righteousness (*ahrāyīh*), (that is) virtuous deeds, for of (all) the things that one may hoard, only righteousness is good.

(3) Do not harbour vengeance in your thoughts lest your enemies catch up with you. (4) Consider rather what injury, harm, and destruction you are liable to suffer by smiting your enemy in vengeance and how you will (perpetually) brood over vengeance in your heart (*vārom*). Do not smite your enemy in vengeance, for it is plain enough that whoever puts vengeance even for a trifling thing out of his mind, will be spared the greatest terrors at the Bridge of the Requiter.[3]

[1]Reading *'ku* for *'kē*.   [3]See below, p. 131.
[2]Text corrupt.

110

(5) Whether you are defendant or plaintiff (at a court of law) tell the truth so that you may be the more certain of acquittal at the trial. (6) For it is clear that by giving true witness a man will be saved, and damned will be the man who perjures himself.[1]

(7) Show moderation in your eating (and drinking) so that you may live long; (8) for moderation in eating (and drinking) is good for the body as moderation in speech is good for the soul. (9) Though a man be very poor in the goods of this world, he is (nevertheless) rich if there is moderation in his character. (10) Pay more attention to your soul than to your belly, for the man who fills his belly usually brings disorder on his spirit.

(11) Take a wife from among your kin so that your lineage may be more protracted; (12) for most of the disorder and vengeful spirit and loss from which the creatures of Ohrmazd have suffered has been caused by the giving of one's daughters ⟨to the sons of strangers⟩ and the asking of the daughters of strangers in marriage for one's sons.[2] So does a family die out.

(13) Abstain rigorously from eating the flesh of kine and all domestic animals (gōspandān) lest you be made to face a strict reckoning in this world and the next; (14) for by eating the flesh of kine and other domestic animals, you involve your hand in sin, and (thereby)[3] think, speak, and do what is sinful; (15) for though you eat but a mouthful(?), you involve your hand in sin, and though a camel be slain by (another) man in another place it is as if you ⟨who eat its flesh⟩ had slain it with your own hand.

(16) Make the traveller welcome so that you yourself may receive a heartier welcome in this world and the next; (17) for he who gives, receives, and (receives) more

---

[1]The text is corrupt but the sense seems certain.
[2]Reading *rādh* for *'nē*. [3]Reading *-ich* for *'chē*.

abundantly. Seat yourself at a banquet where (your host) bids you be seated, for the best place is where a good man sits.

(18) Do not strive for (high) office, for the man who strives for (high) office usually brings disorder on his spirit.

(19) Live in harmony with virtue and do not consent to sin. Be thankful for good fortune and contented in adversity. Avoid an enemy; do not cause harm in doing good works; do not aid and abet evil.

(20) Even should the most fearful calamity befall you, do not doubt concerning the gods and the Religion.

(21) Do not be unduly glad when good fortune attends you, (22) and do not be unduly downcast when misfortune befalls you.

(23) Be contented in adversity, patient in disaster. Do not put your trust in life, but put your trust in good works; (24) for the good man's good works are his advocate and an evil man's ⟨works⟩ are his accuser, (25) and of thoughts, words, and deeds, deeds are the most perfect.

(26) For there is no misfortune which[1] has befallen me, Ādhurbādh, son of Mahraspand, from which I have ⟨not⟩ derived six kinds of comfort. (27) First, when a misfortune ⟨befell me⟩, I was thankful that it was no worse. (28) Secondly, when a misfortune fell not upon my soul but upon my body, (I was thankful), for it seemed better that it should befall the body rather than the soul. (29) Thirdly, (I was thankful) that of all the misfortunes that are due to me[2] one (at least) had passed. (30) Fourthly I was thankful that I was so good a man that the accursed and damnable Ahriman and the demons should bring misfortune on my body on account of my goodness. (31) Fifthly (I was thankful) that since

[1] Reading *'i-m* for *'im*.   [2] Reading *rādh* for *'nē*.

whoever commits an evil deed, will be made to suffer for it either in his own person or in his children, it was I myself who paid the price, not my children. (32) Sixthly, I was thankful that since all the harm that the accursed Ahriman and his demons can do to the creatures of Ohrmazd is limited, any misfortune that befalls me is a loss to Ahriman's treasury, and he cannot inflict it a second time on some other good man.

(33) Abstain rigorously from churlishness, self-will, enmity to the good, anger, rapine, calumny, and lying so that your body be not ill-famed and your soul damned.

(34) Do not plot evil against the evil, for the evil man reaps ⟨the fruit of⟩ his own bad actions. (35) In order to bear with(?) evil men keep the power of goodness in mind and make it your model. (36) Has there ever been a man who associated with evil men who did not regret it in the end?

(37) Do good simply because it is good. Goodness is a real good (*nēvak*) since even evil men extol it. (38) Do whatever you know to be good and do not do anything that you know to be not good. (39) Do not do to others anything that does not seem good to yourself.

(40) Do not underestimate the value of confessing your sins of omission (? *māndak*) to the religious judges, of submitting to the disciplinary whip, and of performing the . . . (?) . . .

(41) You have (only) one name, you are men. Do not pay attention to both the desires (of the body and the soul); (42) for the body and the soul do not both have the same desire. (43) The bodily desires of the body should be satisfied and the soul-desires of the soul.

(44) Never commit a sin out of vengeance, but always strive your utmost to do good works. (45) Do not forsake the righteous law out of lust. (46) Do not violently strike innocent people because you are angry with someone.

(47) Do not be false to a contract out of vengeance lest you be caught up in (the consequences of) your own actions.

(48) Put not your trust in women lest you have cause to be ashamed and to repent. (49) Do not tell your secrets to women lest (all) your toiling be fruitless.

(50) Do not take orders from the crafty lest you meet with ruin. (51) For these four things are most useful to men,[1] wisdom (combined with) courage, vision (combined with) knowledge, wealth (combined with) generosity, and good words (combined with) good deeds. (52) For courage divorced from wisdom is (very) death in a man's body; (53) vision divorced from knowledge is (like) a pictured image of a body; (54) wealth divorced from generosity is like a treasure of Ahriman; (55) good words divorced from good deeds are manifest unbelief (*ahramōghīh*).

(56) The signs of the unbeliever are six; he has the outward appearance of good character, but does the works[2] that beseem a bad character; he performs the liturgy correctly(?), but does evil; he "talks big" to others, but is himself stingy though seeming generous; he is a giver of evil gifts and patient of abuse; his thoughts, words, and deeds do not agree.

(57) Do not say anything that is not specifically of profit except as a joke (*huramīh*), and when joking consider the time and the occasion. (58) For wisdom guards the tongue, the body's fruit is civilized behaviour (*frahang*), and the reward of virtue is Heaven and the receiving and giving of the fruits of the earth; (59) for all forms of courage need wisdom, wisdom knowledge, knowledge experience. To be respected one must have a good name. All actions depend on the proper time and

[1]Reading *'martōmān.   [2]Reading kērōk.

place, while wealth needs to be received and given away, and all enjoyment depends on freedom from fear.

(60) Do not rejoice overmuch when good fortune attends you, and do not grieve overmuch when misfortune overtakes you, (61) for both good fortune and misfortune must befall man. (62) Be grateful to the gods for any good fortune that may befall you in this world and share it with the gods and with good men. Leave (all such things) to the gods, for any reward (that is due to you) will come of its own accord from the place whence it must proceed.

(63) Till the earth and do good, for all men live and are nourished by the tilling of Spandarmat, the Earth.

(64) Do not sin against water, fire, kine, or other domestic animals, or against the dog and the dog species, lest you find the way to Heaven and Paradise (*garōdh-mān*) closed to you.

(65) Do good and keep your doors open to any who may come from far or near, for he who does not do good and does not keep his doors open, will find the door of Heaven and of Paradise closed.

(66) Be zealous in the pursuit of culture (*frahang*), for culture is an adornment in prosperity, a protection in distress, a ready helper in calamity, and becomes a habit in adversity. (67) When you have learnt something, put it into practice, for the man who knows a lot and believes little is the greater sinner. (68) The wisdom of a learned man, if unaccompanied by goodness, turns to injustice (*sāstārīh*) and his intelligence turns to unbelief (*ahra-mōghīh*).

(69) Do not mock at anyone at all, for he who mocks himself becomes the object of mockery, he loses his dignity (*khwarr*) and is execrated, and only rarely will he have a decent and warlike son.

(70) Go every day to wherever good men gather

together to consult them, (71) for whoever goes most frequently to where good men gather together for the purpose of consultation, receives a greater share of virtue and holiness.

(72) Go to the Fire-Temple three times a day and recite the liturgy to the fire, (73) for whoever goes most frequently to the Fire-Temple and recites the liturgy to the fire, receives a greater portion of worldly goods and of holiness.

(74) Keep your body rigorously aloof from the sin[1] of the Lie (sodomy?), from a woman in her menses, and from a harlot in milk so that your soul may not be involved in the hurt such evil does to the body.

(75) Do not leave any sin for which penance is demanded (unconfessed) even for a moment so that the pure Religion of the worshippers of Ohrmazd may not be your enemy.

(76) The body is mortal, but the soul does not pass away.[2] Do good, for the soul (really) is, not the body; spirit (really) is, not matter. (77) Out of respect for the body do not neglect your soul; and do not, out of respect for anyone, forget that the things of this world are transitory. Desire nothing that will bring penance on your body and punishment on your soul.

(78) Do not, out of affection for anyone, neglect the respect due to your soul so that you may not have to suffer a grievous punishment against your will".'

ON THE DRINKING OF WINE
(Mēnōk i Khrat, Anklesaria, 15. 10–18)

'(10) Concerning wine,—it is plain that a good or bad character can be revealed through wine. (11) A man's

[1]Reading bazak.   [2]Reading *asachishn.

goodness is revealed in times of anger and his rationality in times of passion (*varan*) which stirs up unrighteousness; (12) for a man who is assailed by anger and manages to control himself, is shown to be good; and a man who is assailed by passion and manages to control himself, is shown to be reasonable; and a man who is inflamed with wine and manages to control himself, is shown to possess character. This is not a subject for research.

(13) For when a man of good character drinks wine, he is like a gold and silver goblet: the more the light is thrown on it, the more pure and bright does it appear. He becomes more pious in his thoughts, words, and deeds; he is more courtly and sweet with his wife, children, colleagues, and friends, and more energetic in attending to his work and to virtue.

(14) But when a man of bad character drinks wine, he considers himself to be greater than the (just) mean (would allow), he quarrels with his colleagues, is contumacious, speaks calumny and slander. He despises good men, vexes his wife, children, hirelings, slaves, and servants, and spoils the feasting of good men. He banishes peace and introduces contention.

(15) But all men should become sober by drinking wine in moderation. (16) For these several benefits accrue to a man through the drinking of wine in moderation. He digests his food and kindles the (digestive) fire. His wit and intelligence, seed and blood are increased, care is driven away, his colour is heightened, he remembers what he had forgotten, he makes room for goodness in his thoughts; the sight of his eyes and the hearing of his ears and the eloquence of his tongue are increased. He is the more nimble in the despatch of business that needs to be done and seen to; he sleeps sweetly in his bed and rises up from it briskly. And as his reward he wins a fair

name for his body and salvation for his soul and the approval of good men.

(17) And these several defects appear in the man who drinks wine immoderately. (18) His wit and intelligence, seed and blood decrease. He ruins his liver and stores up sickness (for himself); his colour fades and his strength and endurance fail. He neglects his prayers and his praises of the gods. The sight of his eyes and the hearing of his ears and the eloquence of his tongue diminish. He dishonours his food and drink and gives himself up to sloth. He leaves undone all he should say and do. He sleeps with difficulty and rises up listless. And as his reward he causes pain to his own body, his wife and children and friends and relations; he is uncomfortable, suffers a miserable aftermath, and rejoices his enemies. The gods take no pleasure in him; dishonour is the lot of his body and damnation the portion of his soul.'

CHAPTER VIII

SACRAMENTS AND SACRIFICE

NEITHER a mythology nor a code of ethics constitutes the inner core of a religion. This is rather to be found in the ritual, in those symbolical actions which figure forth the religious message which, in the case of Zoroastrianism as of Christianity, is the promise of immortality.

In all religions the great turning-points of life are endowed with a religious significance and blessed by special rites. So in Catholic Christianity birth, the coming of the youth to man's estate, marriage, and death are all solemnized by the appropriate sacrament. So too a man's entry into the priesthood which signifies his dedication to God, is sealed by the sacrament of Holy Orders. Each of these sacraments can, by its very nature, only be received once (except Extreme Unction in cases when death does not immediately supervene). These five sacraments, however, are rather milestones in the religious life : they do not constitute that life itself. This is represented by the two remaining sacraments which, being repeatable an indefinite number of times, *are* the actual spiritual life of the believer. These are the sacraments of penance which revives the soul that was dead in sin, and Holy Communion through which the believer partakes of the divine life itself.

So too in Zoroastrianism we find appropriate ceremonies for birth, puberty, marriage, and death, the four moments in human life that always and everywhere claim the sanction of religion. These, however, are special occasions, and there is no space to deal with them in a book of the present compass. Moreover, readers interested in this subject will find all the information they require in J. J. Modi's *Religious Ceremonies and Customs of the Parsees.*

In this chapter we will concentrate on those two sacraments which can be repeated an unlimited number of times and thereby form the background to the religious life of the pious Zoroastrian. These are penance and the bloodless sacrifice of the *yasna* and the communion in the sacred elements that accompanies it.

Public confession seems to have been the rule in Sassanian Persia, and we still possess versions of the Zoroastrian 'general confession.' Following our usual custom we will now reproduce one of these.

'(3) I confess before the Creator Ohrmazd, before the Amahraspands, before the Good Religion of the worshippers of Ohrmazd, before Mihr, Srōsh, and Rashn,[1] before the spiritual gods and the material gods, before my religious judge and rector, before the immortal *fravahr*[2] of Zoroaster of immortal soul, before my own being (*akhw*), conscience (*dēn*), and soul, and before good men here assembled : in thought, word, and deed I repent, I am sorry, and do penance. . . .

(5) I repent, am sorry, and do penance for any sin I may have committed against Ohrmazd, the Lord, against men, or against mankind. I repent, am sorry, and do penance for any sin I may have committed against Vahuman or against the animal kingdom. I repent, am sorry, and do penance for any sin I may have committed against Artvahisht, the fire, or the different manifestations of fire. I repent, am sorry, and do penance for any

[1] The judges of the soul at death. See below, p. 134.
[2] Man's pre-existent soul. See above, p. 41.

sin I may have committed against Shahrēvar, the metals, or the different manifestations of the metals. I repent, am sorry, and do penance for any sin I may have committed against Spandarmat, the earth, or the earth species. I repent, am sorry, and do penance for any sin I may have committed against Hurdāt, the water, or the different manifestations of the water. I repent, am sorry, and do penance for any sin I may have committed against Amurdāt, the plants, or the different forms of plant life. I repent, am sorry, and do penance for any sin I may have committed against the sacred fires set up in their proper places and particularly against the Farn-bagh, Gushnasp, and Burzēn-Mihr fires.

(6) I repent, am sorry, and do penance for having eaten dead matter, for having swallowed it or buried it or brought it into contact with water or fire, or for having brought water or fire into contact with it. I repent, am sorry, and do penance for having eaten or swallowed waste products of the body, for having buried them or brought them into contact with water or fire, or for having brought water or fire into contact with them. I accept responsibility for every sort (of punishment) which is due to men (who have been polluted) by dead matter and the waste products of the body, and which is due to me too. So numerous are the occasions that I do not know the number of them.

(7) I repent, am sorry, and do penance for not having performed the rite to the Sun, the Moon, and the fire, for not having performed the midday offering, the *gāsānbār* or the *fravartīkān* rites.

(8) I repent, am sorry, and do penance for any sin I may have committed against my superiors, the religious judges and rectors, or the leaders of the Magians. I repent, am sorry, and do penance for any sin I may have committed against my father and mother, sisters and

brothers, wife and children, kith and kin, dwellers in my house, my friends, and (all) others closely connected with me.

(9) I do penance for having talked while eating or drinking. I do penance for having walked with unshod feet. I do penance for having made water on my feet. I do penance for having been false, spoken calumny or slander(?), or for having lied. I do penance for the sins of sodomy, of having intercourse with a woman in her menses, or with a harlot, or with a beast. I do penance for having been guilty of any kind of unlawful intercourse. I do penance for having been proud or overweening, for mockery and vengefulness and lust.

(10) I repent, am sorry, and do penance for all that I ought to have thought and did not think, for all that I ought to have said and did not say, and for all that I ought to have done and did not do. I repent, am sorry, and do penance for all that I ought not to have thought but did think, for all that I ought not to have said but did say, and for all that I ought not to have done but did do.

(11) I repent, am sorry, and do penance for every kind of sin which I have committed against my fellow men, and for those they have committed against me.

I do penance for any sin for which I may have been responsible,—sins which the accursed Destructive Spirit fashioned forth in his enmity to the creatures of Ohrmazd, and which Ohrmazd has declared to be sinful and through which men become sinners and by which they must go to Hell.

(12) I have no doubts concerning the truth and purity of the Good Religion of the worshippers of Ohrmazd, none concerning the Creator, Ohrmazd, and the Amahraspands, the three nights reckoning,[1] or the reality of the

[1]Below, p. 133.

Resurrection and the Final Body. In this religion do I stand, in it I believe without doubting, even as Ohrmazd taught it to Zoroaster, and Zoroaster taught it to Frashōshtar and Jāmāsp, and Ādhurbādh, son of Mahraspand,[1] after submitting to the ordeal and emerging from it victorious, transmitted it in due succession to the righteous religious rectors[2] from whom it came to us. I believe in whatever this religion says or thinks. . . .

(13) This penance have I performed in order to wipe out my sins, in order to obtain my share of reward for good deeds done, and for the comfort of my soul. I have performed it so that the way to Hell may be barred and the way to Heaven opened, (resolved) from now on to sin no more, but to do good works. I have performed it in order to expiate my sins in so far as they need to be expiated and out of love for all that is holy. I dissent from sin and assent to virtue. I am thankful for good fortune and content with (whatever) adversity or misfortune (may befall me). I am content and consent to expiate in the three nights after my death whatever sins have remained unexpiated in the course of my life.[3] Should it happen to me that I leave this world without having done my (final) penance and someone from among my near relations should do penance on my behalf, I agree to it.

In thought, word, and deed I repent, am sorry, and do penance for all the sins for which men can be responsible and for which I have been responsible and the number of which I do not know because they are so numerous.'[4]

The interest in this general confession is not only in

---

[1]See above, p. 98.   [2]I omit two words which are corrupt.
[3]Reading *drang i zhīvishn.   [4]Zand i khwartak Apistāk, pp. 79–84.

the sins confessed but in the order in which they are confessed. We read in the first chapter of this book that Ohrmazd's first spiritual creation was the six Amahraspands, entities which were originally little more than hypostases of himself, but which, in later times, came not only to assume a distinct personality of their own, but to be associated with various classes of natural phenomena on earth. Thus Ohrmazd himself was associated with Man, Vahuman, the Good Mind, with cattle, Artvahisht with fire, Shahrēvar with metals, Spandarmat with the earth, Hurdāt with water, and Amurdāt with plants. All these, then, were the object of particular veneration since they were the visible symbols in the material world of the divine prototypes in Heaven. Thus when sins against these natural objects are mentioned first, it is because to sin against these is equivalent to sinning against their divine patrons, that is to sin against God himself.

The second series of sins relates to dead matter and excreta; and the importance attached by the Zoroastrians to the defilement caused by these seems excessively strange to us. It seems to be based on their curious theory according to which the moment the soul leaves the body, the corpse is occupied and possessed by the demons and is therefore wholly under the control of the powers of evil and thus a source of instantaneous and mortally dangerous defilement. So to bring such matter into contact with the holy elements of fire and water is a terrible sacrilege; it is deliberately to defile a holy thing. It seems to be for this reason that these sins are mentioned first, before the various sins committed against one's fellow men; they are sins against the 'material gods,' against God as he manifests himself in his creation. To defile fire or water is tantamount to joining in Ahriman's attack on God's material creation, it is worse than any sin one can commit against a fellow man, for it is an offence against God himself.

Most of the other sins confessed are parallelled in other religions and correspond to offences against the second five of the Ten Commandments. To the best of my knowledge, however, there is no other religion which accounts talking with one's mouth full or walking unshod to be sinful acts. This can be explained by the emphasis the Zoroastrians lay on good manners and seemly behaviour, an aspect of their religion which emerged clearly from our last chapter. Both these practices are examples of bad behaviour, and for the Zoroastrian there is little difference between the ill-bred person and the sinner.

This text shows that the Zoroastrian believed not only that punishment was due to him for any sin he might commit, but that sins had to be confessed to a priest and the penances he imposed faithfully carried out. If a man died without having fully atoned for his sins, his soul would have to perform the necessary penances during the three nights that elapse between death and judgement, or a near relative could do his penance for him. Confession, then, fulfils much the same role in Zoroastrianism as it does in Catholicism. Sins, in order to be pardoned, have to be confessed, and confession puts the soul once again in a state of grace, restores it to its natural state of friendship with God. Sin, for the Zoroastrian, means the abandonment of man's true dignity which consists in his privileged position of being a front-line soldier freely fighting on the side of Ohrmazd against the wickedness of Ahriman, and enlisting on the side of the latter : it is treason. But it is an act of treason which can be effaced by confession and repentance.

Among Catholics confession is the normal preliminary to Holy Communion, the rite in which the believer partakes of the divine life. In Zoroastrianisn we find a similar rite; and just as in the case of Catholicism the communion takes the form of the consumption of sacred elements which represent the god and which have been previously consecrated and 'immolated' in a bloodless sacrifice, so too, among the Zoroastrians, there is a similar bloodless sacrifice and a similar partaking in the immolated god. The full account of the Zoroastrian *yasna* or sacrifice will be found in chapter XII of Modi's book. Only the briefest possible outline can be given here.

The *yasna* centres round the sacred plant Haoma or Hōm, a plant that originally grew in the Iranian mountains and which apparently had intoxicating qualities. The Haoma, however, is very much more than a plant, it is also a god, the son of Ohrmazd himself. In the sacrifice the Haoma, as plant, is the victim, but as god he is himself the priest. He is at the same time the oblation and the sacrificer, and out of his 'death' comes immortality. Thus when the worshipper partakes of the consecrated Haoma, he partakes of immortality, he obtains a foretaste of the eternal life which will be his in Heaven.

It is strange that the Haoma sacrifice should have become the central sacrificial and sacramental act of the Zoroastrian liturgy, for the cult is far more ancient than Zoroaster since it is found in the sister civilization of the Vedic Indians. Moreover, Zoroaster himself seems to have attacked it, for in his day it was associated with animal sacrifice and probably with much unseemly revelry. The institution of the cult is attributed by him to Yima (later called Yam or Jamshīd) who, according to the earliest tradition, must have been the First Man, a role later filled by Gayōmart. As the following quotations will show, the rite attacked was plainly one in which a bull was slain and its flesh devoured, and in which the Haoma was in all probability consumed.

'Yima,' says Zoroaster, 'son of Vivahvant, is said by tradition to have been one of those sinners, for to gladden men he gave our people portions of a bull to eat.'[1]

Later in the same hymn there is an unmistakable reference to the Haoma, for though the word itself is not used, the term *dūraosha,* the stock epithet of Haoma which means 'he from whom death flees,' appears in the text. The passage is as follows :—

'Long have Grahma and the princes concentrated their attention and energy on impeding him (Zoroaster) in that they are intent on helping the followers of the Lie and in that it is said (among them) that one should burn "him from whom death flees" to help in the slaughter of the bull.'

Here Zoroaster is clearly attacking a form of animal sacrifice which was later to survive in the Mithraic cult which made such sensational progress throughout the Roman Empire. It appears also that the animal sacrifice was accompanied by rites in which the Haoma was used. What is not nearly so clear, however, is that Zoroaster is attacking the Haoma cult as such, rather than an aberrant form of it. Since he uses the word *dūraosha,* 'he from whom death flees,' to describe the Haoma, it seems unlikely that he is attacking the Haoma rite itself as has recently been assumed. If this were so, he would scarcely make use of the epithet which precisely ascribes to the plant the property of conferring immortality. What Zoroaster is actually accusing his enemies of doing is burning the Haoma plant as an accessory rite to the bull sacrifice. He may be speaking metaphorically, and he may only be referring to the inflammation of the senses consequent on the consumption of the intoxicating plant. On the other hand he may merely be protesting at the literal burning of the plant which was not in accord-

[1]Yasna 32.8.

ance with the normal method of extracting its juice by pounding it in a mortar. This verse, then, cannot be used to prove that Zoroaster was opposed to the Haoma rite as such. The two verses quoted, however, do indicate that he was strongly opposed to the sacrifice of bulls or cows and to the association of the Haoma with this.

If this is so, it would go a long way to explain the fact that though animal sacrifice does reappear again and again in later phases of Zoroastrianism and though the god Haoma himself claims the jaws, the tongue, and the left eye of the sacrificial animal,[1] there was always opposition to it on the part of the orthodox. Thus in the Sassanian period we find the name of Ādhurbādh which was synonymous with orthodoxy, associated with a strict vegetarian diet,[2] whereas Yezdigird II who was almost certainly a Zervanite heretic, 'multiplied the sacrifice of white bulls and shaggy he-goats to the fire.'[3]

The question of whether or not animal sacrifice was permissible, then, was not settled until the very end of the Sassanian period. The Haoma rite, however, formed the central part of the Zoroastrian ritual at least from the time of the composition of the younger Avesta. The legitimacy of the rite never seems to have been questioned, and it seems incredible that this should have been so if Zoroaster was himself strongly opposed to it, and not merely to its association with the sacrifice of bulls.

The purpose of the bull sacrifice and the Haoma rite, however, seems to have been the same, namely the winning of immortality. The bull sacrifice was, in addition, a fertility rite, for according to the later mythology all plant life proceeded from the Primal Bull when he was slaughtered by Ahriman. This is not, however, the purpose of the Haoma rite which is the central act of the Zoroastrian *yasna* which, as its name implies, is an

[1] Yasna 11.4.   [2] Above, pp. 72 and 111.   [3] See ZZZ, p. 47.

unbloody 'sacrifice' of the god Haoma who is really present in the plant of that name.

The details of the rite which are, incidentally, extraordinarily interesting for the light they throw on the Mithraic mysteries, have been fully described by Modi. It is only the significance of the rite that concerns us here. The *yasna* is both an 'unbloody sacrifice' and a communion. Besides the Haoma there are other offerings called *myazd* and *drōn,* originally, it seems, liquid and solid offerings. Nowadays the *myazd* is a fruit offering and the *drōn* is 'a flat unleavened round bread made of wheat flour and ghee.'[1] The outward resemblance to the Christian Eucharist is, therefore, striking. Much more striking, however, is the obvious resemblance between the 'bloodless' sacrifice of the Haoma and that of the Catholic Mass. In each case it is the God who is at the same time the victim and the priest,[2] and in each case the offering is made to the Heavenly Father of the priest-victim. When the offering is completed, the flesh of the slain God is consumed by the priest and distributed to the people, and in each case this communion with the God is the elixir of immortality.

The meaning of the rite was abundantly clear to the authors of the Avesta though it seems to have been somewhat rationalized later on. Thus in a later Zoroastrian book the four pressings of the Haoma are likened to the advent of Zoroaster and the coming of his three posthumous sons at the end of time to institute the final Rehabilitation when all men will be made immortal.[3] Yet even in this account the theme of immortality is not lost, and this is the sacramental significance of the Haoma rite. The god is slain,—symbolically pounded in the mortar,—so that man may become immortal. We

[1]Modi, *op. cit.,* p. 279.   [3]*Dātastān i Dēnīk,* ch. 48.
[2]Cf. Yasht 10. 88–90.

shall see in our last chapter how the miraculous Haoma or Hōm is produced in the last days by a final bull-sacrifice which ushers in eternal life. Even though animal sacrifice had been eliminated on earth, it was still allowed to exist in Heaven.

CHAPTER IX

THE INDIVIDUAL JUDGEMENT AT DEATH

In the last chapters we have seen how the Zoroastrian was expected to conduct himself in life, both in his ethical conduct and in the discharge of his ritual obligations. It is now time to consider how he could expect his soul to fare after death. The Zoroastrian doctrine on this subject is absolutely clear. It is based on an original Avestan text, and this text is reproduced, with minor variations, in many of the Pahlavī books. The version reproduced in this chapter is that of the *Mēnōk i Khrat* to which reference has already been made.

There is little that can usefully be said by way of introduction since this text is lucid, graphic, and speaks for itself. Each human soul, on departing this life, hovers for three anxious days in the immediate vicinity of the dead body, and on the fourth day it is required to face the judgement on the 'Bridge of the Requiter,' the bridge of Rashn 'the righteous' who impartially weighs his good and evil deeds. If there is a preponderance of good deeds, the soul is allowed to proceed to Heaven, but if there is a preponderance of evil deeds, it is dragged off to Hell. In case the good and evil deeds are precisely equal, the soul is carried off to a place called *hamēstagān* or 'the place of the mixed.' This is not mentioned in our present text but is referred to many times elsewhere.[1] This place is sometimes compared to Purgatory, but the comparison in inexact, for *hamēstagān* is not a place of purgation but

[1] Cf. ZZZ, pp. 401 and 414.

a place of mild correction in which the only pains suffered are those of heat and cold.[1]

A far closer parallel to the Christian Purgatory is that of the Zoroastrian Hell, for though this is not strictly a place of purgation, it has this much in common with Purgatory, that it is not eternal and that is the prelude to the soul's entrance into Heaven. In the sense that it is a place of torment (which it is), then, it corresponds to the Christian Hell, but in so far as the punishment inflicted on it is only temporary, it corresponds to the Christian Purgatory. The final purgation from the stain of sin takes place at the Last Judgement at the end of time.

And here again there is a close parallel with Christianity; for in both religions the soul is required to face one judgement at death and another universal judgement in the last days when men's bodies are resurrected and reunited with their souls. With the Zoroastrians, however, this final judgement is followed by the final purgation of all men from the stain left behind by sin, and from this all without exception emerge spotless. In Zoroastrianism, then, there is no eternal punishment and all men are finally called upon to enter into Paradise and to contemplate the divine glory. No man is punished eternally for sins committed in time.

The words addressed to the soul of the damned by the demons in Hell are of considerable interest, for they throw some light on the Zoroastrian conception of sin. 'What grieved thee,' they ask, 'in Ohrmazd, the Lord, and the Amahraspands and in fragrant and delightful Heaven, and what grudge or complaint hadst thou of them that thou shouldst come to see Ahriman and the demons and murky Hell; for we will torment thee nor

[1]*Mēnōk i Khrat*, 6.14.

132

shall we have any mercy on thee, and for a long time shalt thou suffer torment.'

Sin, then, when seen from this point of view, is sheer perversity : it is a failure to recognize who is your friend and who is your enemy. The Zoroastrian Religion makes it abundantly clear that God is Man's friend and never under any circumstances causes him suffering for any reason whatsoever. All evil and all suffering proceed from Ahriman. Thus, for a Zoroastrian to admit that God even permits evil is tantamount to attributing to him qualities which are at variance with his nature, and which are indeed proper to Ahriman. It is equivalent to turning God into a demon. The punishment for this is to be delivered over to Ahriman some of whose qualities monotheists are alleged to have attributed to God. This represents a genuine triumph for Ahriman, for besides being the Destroyer, he is also the Deceiver, and his deception takes the form of persuading men that evil proceeds from God. His triumph over individual souls, however, is shortlived, for in the end all human souls, reunited with their bodies, return to Ohrmazd who is their maker and their father.

In this chapter, however, we have only to consider the fate of the individual souls at death; so we let the *Mēnōk i Khrat* speak for itself.

Mēnōk i Khrat, ed. Anklesaria, 1.71–124

'(71) Put not your trust in life, for at the last death must overtake you ; (72) and dog and bird will rend your corpse and your bones will be tumbled on the earth. (73) For for three days and nights the soul sits beside the pillow of the body. (74) And on the fourth day at dawn (the soul) accompanied by the blessed Srōsh, the good

Vāy, and the mighty Vahrām, and opposed by Astvihāt (the demon of death), the evil Vāy, the demon Frēh-zisht and the demon Vizisht, and pursued by the active ill-will of Wrath, the evil-doer who bears a bloody spear, (will reach) the lofty and awful Bridge of the Requiter to which every man whose soul is saved and every man whose soul is damned must come. Here does many an enemy lie in wait. (75) Here (the soul will suffer) from the ill-will of Wrath who wields a bloody spear and from Astvihāt who swallows all creation yet knows no sating, (76) and it will (benefit by) the mediation of Mihr, Srōsh, and Rashn, and will (needs submit) to the weigh-ing (of his deeds) by the righteous Rashn who lets the scales of the spiritual gods incline to neither side, neither for the saved nor yet for the damned, nor yet for kings and princes : (77) not so much as a hair's breadth does he allow (the scales) to tip, and he is no respecter (of persons), (78) for he deals out impartial justice both to kings and princes and to the humblest of men.

(79) And when the soul of the saved passes over that bridge, the breadth of the bridge appears to be one parasang broad. (80) And the soul of the saved passes on accompanied by the blessed Srōsh. (81) And his own good deeds come to meet him in the form of a young girl, more beautiful and fair than any girl on earth. (82) And the soul of the saved says, "Who art thou, for I have never seen a young girl on earth more beautiful or fair than thee." (83) In answer the form of the young girl replies, "I am no girl but thy own good deeds, O young man whose thoughts and words, deeds and religion were good : (84) for when on earth thou didst see one who offered sacrifice to the demons, then didst thou sit (apart) and offer sacrifice to the gods. (85) And when thou didst see a man do violence and rapine, afflict good men and treat them with contumely, and hoard up goods

wrongfully obtained, then didst thou refrain from visiting creatures with violence and rapine of thine own; (86) (nay rather,) thou wast considerate to good men, didst entertain them and offer them hospitality, and give alms both to the man who came from near and to him who came from afar; (87) and thou didst amass thy wealth in righteousness. (88) And when thou didst see one who passed a false judgement or took bribes or bore false witness, thou didst sit thee down and speak witness right and true. (89) I am thy good thoughts, good words, and good deeds which thou didst think and say and do. (90) For though I was venerable (at first), thou hast made me yet more venerable, and though I was honourable (at first), thou hast made me yet more honourable, and though I was endowed with dignity (*khwarrōmand*) (at first), thou hast conferred on me yet greater dignity."

(91) And when the soul departs from thence, then is a fragrant breeze wafted towards him,—(a breeze) more fragrant than any perfume. (92) Then does the soul of the saved ask Srōsh saying, "What breeze is this, the like of which in fragrance I never smelt on earth?" (93) Then does the blessed Srōsh make answer to the soul of the saved, saying, "This is a wind (wafted) from Heaven; hence is it so fragrant."

(94) Then with his first step he bestrides (the heaven of) good thoughts, with his second (the heaven of) good words, and with his third (the heaven of) good deeds; and with his fourth step he reaches the Endless Light where is all bliss. (95) And all the gods and Amahraspands come to greet him and ask him how he has fared, saying, "How was thy passage from those transient, fearful worlds where there is much evil to these worlds which do not pass away and in which there is no adversary, O young man whose thoughts and words, deeds and religion are good?"

(96) Then Ohrmazd, the Lord, speaks, saying, "Do not ask him how he has fared, for he has been separated from his beloved body and has travelled on a fearsome road." (97) And they served him with the sweetest of all foods, even with the butter of early spring so that his soul may take its ease after the three nights terror of the Bridge inflicted on him by Astvihāt and the other demons, (98) and he is sat upon a throne everywhere bejewelled.

(99) For it is revealed that the sweetest of all foods offered by the spiritual gods to man or woman after the parting of consciousness and body is always the butter of early spring, and that they seat him on a throne everywhere bejewelled. (100) And for ever and ever he dwells with the spiritual gods in all bliss for evermore.

(101) But when the man who is damned dies, for three days and nights does his soul hover near his head and weeps, saying, "Whither shall I go and in whom shall I now take refuge?" (102) And during those three days and nights he sees with his eyes all the sins and wickedness that he committed on earth. (103) On the fourth day the demon Vizarsh comes and binds the soul of the damned in most shameful wise, and despite the opposition of the blessed Srōsh drags it off to the Bridge of the Requiter. (104) Then the righteous Rashn makes clear to the soul of the damned that it is damned (indeed).

(105) Then the demon Vizarsh seizes upon the soul of the damned, smites it and ill-treats it without pity, urged on by Wrath. (106) And the soul of the damned cries out with a loud voice, makes moan, and in supplication makes many a piteous plea; much does he struggle though his life-breath endures no more. (107) When all his struggling and his lamentations have proved of no avail, no help is proffered him by any of the gods nor yet by any of the demons, but the demon Vizarsh drags him off against his will into nethermost Hell.

(108) Then a young girl who yet has no semblance of a young girl, comes to meet him. (109) And the soul of the damned says to that ill-favoured wench, "Who art thou? for I have never seen an ill-favoured wench on earth more ill-favoured and hideous than thee." (110) And in reply that ill-favoured wench says to him, "I am no wench, but I am thy deeds,—hideous deeds,—evil thoughts, evil words, evil deeds, and an evil religion. (111) For when on earth thou didst see one who offered sacrifice to the gods, then didst thou sit (apart) and offer sacrifice to the demons. (112) And when thou didst see one who entertained good men and offered them hospitality, and gave alms both to those who came from near and to those who came from afar, then didst thou treat good men with contumely and show them dishonour, thou gavest them no alms and didst shut thy door (upon them). (113) And when thou didst see one who passed a just judgment or took no bribes or bore true witness or spoke up in righteousness, then didst thou sit down and pass false judgement, bear false witness, and speak unrighteously. (114) I am thy evil thoughts, evil words, and evil deeds which thou didst think and say and do. (115) For though I was disreputable (at first), thou hast made me yet more disreputable; and though I was dishonourable (at first), thou hast made me yet more dishonourable, and though I sat (at first) among the unaware, thou didst make me yet more unaware."

(116) Then with his first step he goes to (the hell of) evil thoughts, with his second to (the hell of) evil words, and with his third to (the hell of) evil deeds. And with his fourth step he lurches into the presence of the accursed Destructive Spirit and the other demons. (117) And the demons mock at him and hold him up to scorn, saying, "What grieved thee in Ohrmazd, the Lord, and the Amahraspands and in fragrant and delightful Heaven,

and what grudge or complaint hadst thou of them that thou shouldst come to see Ahriman and the demons and murky Hell? for we will torment thee nor shall we have any mercy on thee, and for a long time shalt thou suffer torment."

(118) And the Destructive Spirit cries out to the demons, saying, "Ask not concerning him, for he has been separated from his beloved body and has come through that most evil passage-way; (119) but serve him (rather) with the filthiest and most foul food that Hell can produce."

(120) Then they bring him poison and venom, snakes and scorpions and other noxious reptiles (that flourish) in Hell, and they serve him with these to eat. (121) And until the Resurrection and the Final Body he must remain in Hell, suffering much torment and many kinds of chastisement. (122) And the food that he must for the most part eat there is all, as it were, putrid and like unto blood.

(123) The Spirit of Innate Wisdom said to the wise man, "Lo, this is what thou didst ask concerning the maintenance of the body and the salvation of the soul, and (now) thou hast been told by me and art well instructed therein. (124) Pay great attention (to this instruction) and put it into practise; for this is thy highest path for the maintenance of thy body and the salvation of thy soul".'

CHAPTER X

THE RESURRECTION OF THE BODY AND LIFE EVERLASTING

As we have already seen, for the Zoroastrians as for the Christians the individual judgement of the soul at death is only a prelude to the final judgement at the end of time when the body is resurrected and reunited with the soul. The Zoroastrian tradition is, however, more logical than the Christian, for whereas in Christianity God's eternal sentence on the human soul which was irrevocably fixed when it passed from this life on earth, is merely confirmed at the Last Judgement, 'the day of wrath when even the just are scarcely secure,' for the Zoroastrian the last reckoning, if such it can be called, is merely the prelude to the three days purgation in molten metal after which the damned emerge from Hell and the whole human race without any exception is united in heaven where it will praise God for evermore. God does not condemn his creatures to eternal torment for sins, however terrible, committed in time. These are punished, and punished severely, in a temporal Hell over which Ahriman and his demons preside; but no *good* God could mete out eternal punishment to his creatures, however grave their sins, for this would be contrary both to his goodness and to his justice. To suppose otherwise is to attribute qualities to God which properly belong to the Devil; and for the Zoroastrian this is the crassest blasphemy. The Yahweh of the Old Testament, in his fury, is as repugnant to him as is the arbitrary Allah of the

Koran. The Zoroastrian God truly tempers justice with mercy : he has no 'terrible' side, and least of all is he capable of 'wrath,' a quality personified by the Zoroastrians as the demon Ēshm who, under Ahriman, is with Āz, the demon of Concupiscence, the most redoubtable as well as the most pernicious of the entire demonic host.

Thus the final Resurrection, the *Frashkart* or 'Rehabilitation,' is not so much a final judgement as a time when all things shall be restored and when all will once again be very good. It is the final triumph of Ohrmazd over Ahriman, of the principle of good over the principle of evil when the latter is made powerless for ever and ever.

The text we reproduce in this chapter is that of the *Bundahishn* on which we have already drawn extensively. The *Frashkart* or final Rehabilitation of Ohrmazd's creation and definitive expulsion of Ahriman and his hordes is a favourite topic with the authors of the Pahlavī books. It is treated at length by both Mānush-chihr and his brother Zātspram who lived in the ninth century A.D. The first of these gives us a very detailed and fully orthodox account of the last days, while the second unfolds a version which shows traces of Zervanite heresy. Besides these there are two other full scale accounts, one in the Pahlavī Rivāyats or 'Traditions,' and the other in the so-called *Bahman Yasht*. I have selected the version of the *Bundahishn* first because it is relatively succinct, secondly because the text is less complex than that of Mānushchihr though the latter might well claim to have a greater orthodox authority, and thirdly because it is free from the mass of heterogeneous mythological material which causes confusion in many of the other accounts and which is therefore unsuitable in a book which is designed for a wide public. The versions of both Mānushchihr and Zātspram are undoubtedly superior as literary productions, but the *Bundahishn* gives all the essentials of this final drama in the battle of good and evil in a shorter compass, and thereby nicely rounds off these selections from the Zoroastrian texts which are intended to present the reader with all the essential doctrines of the Zoroastrians, with their theory and practice, their cosmology and eschatology. Moreover, Zātspram's account which has a broad dignity suitable to the grandiose theme of the overthrow of evil and the resurrection of all things in everlasting life, has already been adequately edited and translated elsewhere.[1]

We have already noticed[2] that in the text from the *Bundahishn* which describes the behaviour of the first human couple, the eating of food seems to be regarded as sinful. Similarly, in our present text, the gradual abandonment of the habit of eating is represented as leading to immortality; for only so can the power of the demon Āz, who is Concupiscence and Gluttony, be overcome. I have devoted considerable space to the demon Āz elsewhere,[3] but only in connexion with the Zervanite heresy. In orthodox Zoroastrianism it seems to be equally true that Āz, conceived of as 'gluttony' rather than as the more comprehensive 'concupiscence,' is the demon who ultimately causes death and is therefore the prime obstacle to the attainment of immortality.

The fact that bodily life can only be sustained by the consumption of food, that is by taking other lives and assimilating them into the bodily system, did not escape the Zoroastrians. The body which must die is characterized by the corollary fact that it must eat, and this process is that whereby Āz lives and has her being. In the last days, however, when the power of Ahriman and

[1]ZZZ, pp. 348–54.   [2]pp. 70–1.   [3]ZZZ, pp. 166–83.

his demons is greatly reduced, man is enabled to live on practically nothing, and this in turn deprives Āz of her normal sustenance. Finally man is able to do without food and drink altogether. The *Bundahishn* does not follow the account given by Zātspram according to which Āz, deprived of her normal sustenance, proceeds to devour the other demons and threatens to eat up Ahriman himself. This version was, perhaps, peculiar to Zervanism, for the more orthodox versions know nothing of it. In the *Bundahishn,* at any rate, Ahriman is spared this final indignity and Āz is left to pine slowly away.

In the *Bundahishn* the final Resurrection seems to precede the overthrow of Ahriman and the demons whereas in Zātspram it follows after it. The hero of the drama of the resurrection of the body is Sōshyans, the last of the posthumous sons of Zoroaster, who arise in the last three millennia of finite time to bring about the Rehabilitation. His name is conventionally translated as 'the Saviour' : more literally it means 'he who will bring benefit' and this is clearly reflected in the Pahlavī translation *sūtōmand* which means 'the beneficial or profitable one.' His function it is to raise men's bodies from the elements into which they had been dissolved and to reunite them with their souls. This done, the resurrected have to endure a three days ordeal by molten metal, the final punishment which the damned have to endure before they too are called upon to share in the bliss which is the ultimate destiny of all mankind. The ordeal causes no discomfort to those who are already saved, for the surging metal seems to them like warm milk ; but the damned must experience the full rigour and reality of the torment.

The whole of mankind is now finally purified from all taint and stain of past wrong-doing, but they have yet to receive bodily immortality. This is, strangely enough, brought about by one last animal sacrifice performed by Sōshyans himself. The bull Hadhayans is ritually immolated and from its fat the white Hōm or Haoma is prepared, that same liquid which the faithful had received sacramentally on earth as an earnest of immortality and which they now receive in truth as the elixir of eternal life.

Sōshyans, being born of the seed of Zoroaster, is a hero, not a god. It is then a gracious act of divine courtesy to the human race that he should be entrusted with the final rehabilitation of the world and the resurrection of the dead. God wills that the bodily resurrection of the human race should be entrusted to one of its own kind. Sōshyans is in full charge of this human drama, and Ohrmazd and his divine associates only intervene to settle their own accounts with Ahriman, the Fiend, and his abominable brood. Each of the Amahraspands seizes upon his own predestined enemy and destroys him. Finally there remain only Ahriman and Āz. It is now Ohrmazd's turn to hold a great sacrifice, this time to ensure the utter defeat of Ahriman and Āz. Once the sacrifice is completed the unholy pair are swallowed up in the 'darkness and gloom' from which they should never have emerged. Ahriman 'is laid low and made unconscious so that he will never again arise from that low estate. There have been some who have said that he will be forever powerless and, as it were, slain, and that neither the Destructive Spirit nor his creation will exist.'[1]

The accounts in the Pahlavī books which describe the final overthrow of Ahriman seem uncertain as to whether his overthrow means his actual annihilation or not. On balance it would seem that the orthodox view was that since he is, by definition, a substance, he cannot be actually reduced to nothing. He is, however, by the

[1]ZZZ, p. 355.

unanimous consent of all our sources, reduced to absolute powerlessness. His position seems to be analogous to that of the human body at death : he is not destroyed but disintegrates into unconscious and inoperative atoms which have no power of reintegrating themselves into a unified being with any power to act. Thus there can be no possibility of Ahriman's resuming his aggression against the reconstituted world.

As Ahriman and Āz are annihilated the 'serpent Gōchihr,' the mysterious demon who infests the sky during the 'mixed state,' falls on to the earth, and is finally burnt up in the flood of molten metal in which the human race has been purged. The good creation is now delivered forever from all adversity and opposition, and lives eternally in a state of bliss with Ohrmazd and the gods.

Throughout this little book we have seen how extremely common-sense and earthy the Zoroastrians try to be. Their conception of Heaven is no exception to this rule. Heaven is simply a return to the earthly state of affairs which existed before Ahriman had the madness to attack. It is like a huge family reunion in which an ideal earthly life is restored, a life that centres round the human family and where the husband may once again enjoy the intimate fellowship of his lawful wife and the company of his sons and daughters. Life in Heaven is the natural perfection of life on earth where the body enjoys its natural pleasures, except that, being immortal, it no longer desires to eat, and where the soul gives praise with a loud voice to Ohrmazd and the Amahraspands. There the whole human family united forever lives in everlasting bliss.

'On the Raising of the Dead and the Final Body

(1) It is said in the Religion that just as Mashyē and Mashyānē, after they had grown out of the earth, consumed water first, then plants, then milk, and then meat,[1] so do men when they ⟨are about to⟩ die, abstain first from the eating of meat and milk and then from bread; but right up to the moment of death they drink water.

(2) So too in the millennium of Oshētarmāh[2] the power of Āz (gluttony) is so diminished that men are satisfied by eating one meal every three days and nights. After that they abstain from eating meat, and eat (only) plants and the milk of domestic animals. After that they abstain from drinking milk also; then they abstain from eating plants too, and drink only water. Ten years before the coming of Sōshyans they reach a state in which they eat nothing, yet do not die.

(3) Then Sōshyans will raise up the dead, as (the Religion) says, "Zoroaster asked Ohrmazd, 'From whence can the body which the wind has carried off and the water swept away, be put together again; and how will the raising of the dead come to pass?' And Ohrmazd made answer (and said): 'When ⟨I established⟩ the sky without pillar on an invisible (*mēnōk*) support, its ends flung wide apart, bright with the substance of shining metal, and when I created the earth which supports the whole material creation though itself has no material support, and when I set the Sun, Moon, and stars,—forms of light,—on their courses in the atmosphere, and when I created grain on earth and scattered it abroad so

---

[1] See, above, pp. 77ff.
[2] The last millennium before the coming of Sōshyans.

that it grows up again and yields a greater crop, and
when I created various and variegated colours in the
plants, and when I gave fire to the plants and other
things and it did not burn (them), and when I created
the embryo in its mother's womb and gave it nourishment, giving to it its several organs,—hair and skin and
nails and blood, tendons and eyes and ears and other
organs, and when I gave feet to the water so that it could
run forward, and when I created the clouds on high
(*mēnōkīk*) to carry away the waters from the earth and
to rain them down wheresoever they would, and when I
created the atmosphere (*vāy*) which blows through the
power of the wind upwards and downwards as it wills,
and this is visible to the eye though it cannot be seized
by the hand,—when I created each one of these things,
each was more difficult than the raising of the dead. For
in the raising of the dead I have the assistance of the
likes of these. When they were still ⟨uncreated⟩, I had
⟨no such assistance⟩.

(4) Behold! If I created what had not been, why
should it be impossible for me to recreate what once was?
For at that time I shall demand from the Spirit of the
Earth the bones, from the water the blood, from the
plants the hair, from the wind the spirit (*jān*) even as
they received them at the primal creation'."

(5) First will be raised the bones of Gayōmart, then the
bones of Mashyē and Mashyānē : then will the bones of
(all) other men be raised up. For fifty-seven years will
Sōshyans raise the dead and all men will be resurrected,
both those who were saved and those who were damned.
And each man will arise in the place where his spirit left
him or where first he fell to the ground.

(6) And when the gods have restored to the whole of
the material creation its proper form and shape, then
will they give (men) their proper character (*adhvēnak*).

And of the light that is with the Sun half will they give to Gayōmart and half to the rest of men.

(7) Then will men recognize each other, that is, soul will recognize soul and body body (thinking), "This is my father," or "This is my brother," or "This is my wife," or "This is whatever close relative it may be." Then the assembly of Isat-vāstar will convene when men stand upon the earth in that assembly; and every man will see his good and evil deeds, and the saved will be as clearly distinguished from the damned as is a white sheep from a black.

(8) And in that assembly the damned man who had on earth a friend who was saved, will upbraid the man who was saved, saying, "Why didst thou not apprise me on earth of the good deeds that thou thyself wast doing?" And if in truth the man who was saved did not so apprise him, then must he needs be put to shame in that assembly.

(9) Then will they separate the saved from the damned, and carry off the saved to Paradise (*garōdhmān*) and hurl the damned back into Hell; and for three days and nights these denizens of Hell will endure punishment in Hell, in their bodies and in their souls (*jān*) while the saved experience joy in their bodies during their three days and nights in Paradise.

(10) For it is said that on that day when damned is separated from saved, and saved from damned, tears will flow down from (the eyes of) all men, right down to their feet. When son is separated from the company of father, brother from brother, friend from friend, then will every man bewail the deeds he did, the saved weeping for the damned, and the damned weeping for themselves. It may be the father who is saved and the son who is damned, or it may be one brother who is saved and the other who is damned.

(11) Those who committed sins of their own free will(?)[1] like Dahāk and Āfrāsyāb and Vātan(?) and others of this kind who committed mortal sin, will endure the *vamad-adhvēnak*(??) punishment, but no man will have to endure the punishment called *tishrām khshafnām* (the full three nights punishment).

(12) At that time when the final Rehabilitation is brought about, fifteen men and fifteen maidens from among those blessed men of whom it is written that they are (still) alive, will come to the assistance of Sōshyans.

(13) And Gōchihr, the serpent in the heavenly sphere, will fall from the summit of the Moon to the earth, and the earth will suffer pain like unto the pain a sheep feels when a wolf rends out its wool.

(14) Then will the Fire-god and the god Airyaman melt the metals that are in the mountains and hills, and they will flow over the earth like rivers. And they will make all men to pass through that molten metal and (thereby) make them clean. And it will seem to him who was saved as if he were walking through warm milk, but to the man who was damned it will seem exactly like walking through molten metal.

(15) Then will all men come together in the greatest joy, father and son, brothers and all friends. And one man will ask another, "How has thy soul fared in all these many years? Wast thou saved, or wast thou damned?" Next the soul will see its body, will question it and be answered by it.

(16) All men will become of one voice and give praise with a loud voice to Ohrmazd and the Amahraspands. At this time Ohrmazd will have brought his creation to its consummation, and there will be no (further) work he need do.

(17) While the resurrection of the dead proceeds,

[1] Text corrupt.

148

Sōshyans and his helpers will perform the sacrifice of the raising of the dead, and in that sacrifice the bull Hadhayans will be slain, and from the fat of the bull they will prepare the white Hōm (Haoma), (the drink of) immortality, and give it to all men. And all men will become immortal for ever and ever.

(18) This too is said, that men who had reached middle age will be resurrected as (men of) forty years of age; and those who died young and before their prime will be resurrected as (lads of) fifteen years of age.

(19) To each man his wife and children will be restored, and they will have intercourse with their wives even as they do on earth to-day, but no children will be born to them.

(20) Then at the behest of the Creator Sōshyans will distribute to all men their wages and reward in accordance with their deeds. Some there are who are so blessed that he says, "Take them to the Paradise of Ohrmazd as is their due." They will take up their bodies, and for ever and ever they will walk together with them.

(21) And this too is said, that whoso (on earth) had not performed the sacrifice nor ordered a *gētōkhrīt* ("earthly redemption") nor given clothing in alms to those who deserved it, (will stand) there naked, and Ohrmazd will perform sacrifice on his behalf and the Spirit of the Gāthās will provide him with raiment.

(22) Then Ohrmazd will seize hold of the Destructive Spirit, Vahuman (the Good Mind) will seize Akōman (the Evil Mind), Artvahisht Indar, Shahrēvar Sāvul, Spandarmat Tarōmat (Arrogance) who is Nānghaith, Hurdāt and Amurdāt will seize Tairich and Zairich, True Speech False Speech, and the blessed Srōsh will seize upon Ēshm (Wrath) of the bloody banner.

(23) Then (only) two Lies will remain, Ahriman and Āz (Concupiscence). Ohrmazd will come (down) to

149

earth, himself the "Zōt"-priest with the blessed Srōsh as his "Rāspīk"-priest, and he will hold the sacred girdle in his hand. By that Gāthic ritual Ahriman and Āz, their weapons smashed, will be made powerless; and by the same passage through the sky by which they rushed in, they will hurtle into the darkness and gloom.

(24) And the serpent Gōchihr will be burnt up in the molten metal; and the molten metal will flow out into Hell. And (all) the stench and corruption that was in Hell will be burnt up by this molten metal and made clean. And ⟨the hole in(?)⟩ Hell by which the Destructive Spirit rushed in, will be sealed up[1] by that molten metal, and the earth that was in Hell will be brought up to the broad expanse of (this) material world.

(25) Then will the final Resurrection take place in the two worlds; and in accordance with its own desire the material world will become immortal for ever and ever.

(26) This too is said, that this earth will become flat, with neither hills nor dales. There will be neither mountains nor ridges nor pits, neither high ground nor low.'

[1]Reading *'hanbāsht.

SELECT BIBLIOGRAPHY

I. SOURCES IN TRANSLATION:

The Sacred Books of the East series (Clarendon Press, now re-issued by Motilal Banarsidass, Delhi) contains both the *Avesta* (vols. iv, xxiii, and xxxi) and most of the Pahlavī books (vols. v, xviii, xxiv, xxvii, and xlvii). All are sadly out of date.

More modern translations of individual works are:

Bahram T. Anklesaria, *Zand-Ākāsīh, Iranian or Greater Bundahišn*. Bombay, 1956.

—, *Vichitakiha-i Zatsparam*. Bombay, 1964.

—, *The Pahlavī Rivāyat of Āturfarnbag and Farnbag-Srōš*. Bombay, 1969.

M. Boyce, *The Letter of Tansar*. Rome, 1968.

Ervad M. F. Kanga, *Čītak Handarz i Pōryōtkešān*. Bombay, 1960.

P. M. F. Kotwal, *The Supplementary Texts of the Šayest nē-šayast*. Copenhagen, 1969.

J. de Menasce, *Le troisième livre du Dēnkart*. Paris, 1973.

—, *Škand-gumānīk vičār*. Fribourg, 1945.

II. SOME BOOKS SUITABLE FOR THE GENERAL READER:

H. W. Bailey, *Zoroastrian Problems in the Ninth Century Books*, 2nd ed. Oxford, 1971.

E. Benveniste, *The Persian Religion according to the Chief Greek Texts*. Paris, 1929.

L. C. Casartelli, *The Philosophy of the Mazdayasnian Religion under the Sassanids*, tr. Jamasp Asa. Bombay, 1889.

A. Christensen, *L'Iran sous les Sassanides*, 2nd ed. Copenhagen, 1944.

J. Duchesne-Guillemin, *Zoroastre*. Paris, 1948.

—, *The Hymns of Zarathustra*, tr. M. Henning. London, 1952.

—, *Ormazd et Ahriman*. Paris, 1953.

—, *La religion de l'Iran ancien*. Paris, 1962. Eng. tr. K. M. Jamasp Asa, *Religion of Ancient Iran*. Bombay, 1973.

L. H. Gray, *The Foundations of the Iranian Religions*. Bombay, 1925.

W. B. Henning, *Zoroaster, Politician or Witch-doctor?*. Oxford, 1951.

A. V. W. Jackson, *Zoroastrian Studies*. New York, 1928, and reprints.

R. P. Masani, *The Religion of the Good Life*. London, 1938.

J. J. Modi, *The Religious Ceremonies and Customs of the Parsees*, 2nd ed. Bombay, 1937.

M. Molé, *Culte, mythe et cosmologie dans l'Iran ancien*. Paris, 1963.

J. H. Moulton, *Early Zoroastrianism*. London, 1913, and reprint 1972.

J. D. C. Pavry, *The Zoroastrian Doctrine of the Future Life*. New York, 1929.

R. C. Zaehner, *Zurvan, A Zoroastrian Dilemma*. Oxford, 1955. Reprint Biblo and Tanner, New York, 1972.

—, *The Dawn and Twilight of Zoroastrianism*. London, 1961 (reprinting).

INDEX

153